PENGUIN PASSN

*Pygmalion*

Vivian Summers was educated at the universities of Exeter and
Cambridge. He was Head of the English Department at Queen
Elizabeth School, Crediton, for over thirty years. He has also
lectured at a college of education and at the International Summer
Schools held at Exeter University. He is currently an examiner, a
lecturer and a freelance writer with several books on English to his
credit.

PENGUIN PASSNOTES

BERNARD SHAW

# *Pygmalion*

VIVIAN SUMMERS
ADVISORY EDITOR: S. H. COOTE, M.A., PH.D.

PENGUIN BOOKS

Penguin Books Ltd, Harmondsworth, Middlesex, England
Viking Penguin Inc., 40 West 23rd Street, New York, New York 10010, U.S.A.
Penguin Books Australia Ltd, Ringwood, Victoria, Australia
Penguin Books Canada Limited, 2801 John Street, Markham, Ontario, Canada L3R 1B4
Penguin Books (N.Z.) Ltd, 182–190 Wairau Road, Auckland 10, New Zealand

First published 1986

Permission to reproduce *Pygmalion* in non-dramatic form given by
The Society of Authors – The Society of Authors on behalf of the Bernard Shaw Estate.

Made and printed in Great Britain by
Richard Clay (The Chaucer Press) Ltd, Bungay, Suffolk
Typeset in Monophoto Ehrhardt by
Northumberland Press Ltd, Gateshead

*The publishers are grateful to the following Examination Boards for permission to reproduce
questions from examination papers used in individual titles in the Passnotes series:*

*Northern Ireland Schools Examination Council, University of Oxford Delegacy of Local
Examinations, Welsh Joint Education Committee.*

*The Examination Boards accept no responsibility for the accuracy or method of working in
any suggested answers given as models.*

# *Contents*

# To the Student

This book is designed to help you with your O-level, C.S.E. or 16+ English Literature examinations. It contains an introduction to the life of Shaw and to the background of the play, analysis of scenes and characters, and a commentary on some of the issues raised by the play. References are to the Penguin edition of *Pygmalion*, edited by Dan H. Laurence.

When you use this book remember that it is no more than an aid to your study. It will help you find passages quickly and perhaps give you some ideas for essays. But remember: *This book is not a substitute for reading the play and it is your response and your knowledge that matter.* These are the things the examiners are looking for, and they are also the things that will give you the most pleasure. Show your knowledge and appreciation to the examiner, and show them clearly.

# Introduction

## THE LIFE OF BERNARD SHAW

Shaw was born in Dublin on 26 July 1856. Like the Eynsford Hills in *Pygmalion*, his family had a claim to being gentry without the income to support the position. Shaw's father lacked the money to start a career in business or in one of the professions and worked for some time as a clerk in the Law Courts. He added to his difficulties by drinking heavily. Later, when his post at the Courts was done away with, he converted his pension into a lump sum and went into partnership as a wholesale corn merchant.

His wife was a woman of considerably more spirit and accomplishment. She had three children – Shaw having two elder sisters. While he was still a small boy, his mother sought an outlet for her energies away from the stifling atmosphere of an impoverished but genteel home. She found it in music. Possessor of a promising voice and one she considered worth training, Mrs Shaw took lessons from a singing teacher named George John Lee, who lived near by.

In keeping with their genteel background, the Shaws at first had their son educated by a governess. Shaw did not go to school until he was eleven and then the experience was not a very happy one. Altogether he attended four schools until the end of his formal education at the age of fifteen. The most valuable part of his education came from his own wide reading. Furthermore, he benefited from the artistic friends who gathered around his mother and her singing teacher. Their lively discussions about the arts opened his mind to ways of life and attitudes very different from those of his befuddled father. Above all, he developed a considerable knowledge of music, which he later turned to professional use as a critic.

George Lee virtually became a member of the family when he

moved in with the Shaws and Shaw himself was impressed by the man and his forthright views. When Lee later went to London, it was an event that was ultimately to lead Shaw himself to leave Dublin and settle in England.

When he left school, Shaw found work in a Dublin estate agent's office. At the age of sixteen he was made cashier as a temporary replacement for an employee who had run off with some of the firm's money. Shaw filled the post so well that he was given the job permanently. He stayed with the firm until he was twenty. By this time his interest in literature and the theatre had grown considerably. He frequently went to plays and concerts in Dublin and had ambitions to be a writer, but prospects for such a career seemed limited in Ireland and so he began to think of moving to London.

The move was made easier for Shaw because his mother, following rapidly in George Lee's footsteps, had taken her daughter Agnes to London and was earning her living there as a singing teacher. Shaw arrived in London in 1876 but fame and fortune lay many years ahead. He found no regular employment for nearly ten years and remained dependent on his mother. But for her he might have followed the classic road of a struggling artist and either starved or given up his literary ambitions. As it was, he was able to write, to widen his education and to make important friends.

Shaw's writing varied from jobs as menial as producing verses to accompany printers' illustration blocks to writing no less than five novels. No publisher was interested in his books which only found their way into print very much later when his fame as a playwright was established. Despite lack of encouragement, Shaw persevered as a writer, setting himself the task of writing a definite number of words every day.

Shaw's way of life left him plenty of time for study and he applied himself to this with typical energy. The Reading Room of the British Museum was a favourite haunt and there he read and pondered deeply on contemporary social problems. He undertook a thorough study of the works of the founder of Communism, Karl Marx, and also maintained and extended his interest in music. His friend, the writer William Archer, once found him in the British Museum with two large books open before him – one a volume by Karl Marx, the other a score of a Wagner opera!

The revolutionary ideas of Socialism were exciting many thinking people at this time and Shaw was among them. The Fabian Society, which became the intellectual power-house of Socialism, was founded in 1884 and Shaw was among its first members. Its call for social justice and equality appealed enormously to Shaw and he devoted much of his life to showing up the weaknesses, inadequacies and injustices of English society. He set out his views in great detail in *The Intelligent Woman's Guide to Socialism and Capitalism*, a work to which he devoted many years and which was finally published in 1928.

His interest in Socialism brought him into contact with leading figures in the movement and he came to be accepted as one himself. Much in demand as a speaker, despite his ready wit and wealth of stimulating ideas he at first suffered badly from nerves. He therefore forced himself to accept every invitation to speak so as to overcome his fears. He also took elocution lessons from an Alsatian singing teacher named Richard Deck, a point of interest when one thinks of Eliza's lessons in *Pygmalion.*

It is remarkable that the man who was to become the outstanding British playwright of the twentieth century did not write a play until he was thirty-six years old. By this time his fortunes as a writer had improved. William Archer had introduced him to the editor of the *Pall Mall Gazette* and Shaw soon became a member of the reviewing staff. Prepared to turn his hand to anything – books, art, plays or music – he became music critic of the *Star* and established a reputation that has lasted to the present day as one of the really outstanding writers on the contemporary musical scene. Later, he also became a drama critic.

His interest in writing plays came about through his involvement with Socialism. For a long time Shaw did not see the theatre of the day as being relevant to the development of his own ideas, but controversy over the plays of the Norwegian dramatist, Henrik Ibsen, made him consider the stage as a platform for serious themes. In 1890 he delivered a famous lecture for the Fabian Society which he later used as the basis for his book *The Quintessence of Ibsenism.*

He saw in the work of Ibsen the new idea of presenting contemporary problems that affected real people and the playwright's readiness to let his characters 'sit down and discuss'. Both these characteristics appealed greatly to Shaw and he had the opportunity to put them into practice when, in 1892, he heard that a new and forward-looking management called The Independent Theatre Company was looking for new plays. He revised a half-written script that he and Archer had begun and abandoned some years before and it was given two performances. This was *Widowers' Houses*; Shaw called it his 'first and worst play'. It dealt with the sufferings of slum dwellers exploited by middle-class owners. The play was not well received but Shaw was excited by the possibilities of using the theatre for this new kind of play and he continued to write.

Success was slow in coming, even if the list of plays written in the 1890s which contained such now-famous titles as *Arms and the Man*, *Candida* and *You Never Can Tell* suggests otherwise. However, a few years later, in 1904, six performances of *Candida* at the Royal Court Theatre in London proved such a success that the actor-manager Granville Barker (who was enthusiastic about Shaw's plays) ran a number of seasons of modern drama at the theatre. These included new plays by Shaw, among them *Man and Superman* and *The Doctor's Dilemma*.

By the time these seasons ended in 1907, Shaw was undoubtedly the leading playwright of the new English drama. He continued to write prolifically and, by the time *Pygmalion* was written in 1912, he had produced twenty-eight plays in his first twenty years as a dramatist. Many more plays lay ahead, including two which are regarded as his finest, *Heartbreak House* (1917) and *St Joan* (1923). In 1929 a drama festival was founded in Malvern at which Shaw's plays were the principal feature. For the first festival he wrote *The Apple Cart*.

Shaw was now seventy-three but he continued to write and produce a dozen or more plays, some of them quite short. He also wrote many articles and contributed extra scenes to the film of his play *Caesar and Cleopatra*. When he was eighty-three he wrote 'In Good King Charles's Golden Days', a lively and amusing conversation piece that recalled the sparkle of his earlier plays.

Shaw's domestic life was fairly uneventful. He did not marry Charlotte Payne-Townshend until he was forty-two. She was a wealthy woman who supported the Socialist cause and wanted to devote herself and her money to assisting a man of promise in his career. She was introduced to Shaw, they became friends and were eventually married. They agreed not to have children, but Charlotte provided Shaw with a comfortable and stable home life. She lived to the age of eighty-six; Shaw outlived her by seven years.

As Shaw's career developed, he became famous not only in England but around the world. In his later years he went abroad frequently, usually at the insistence of his wife who enjoyed travelling far more than he did. He visited, among other countries, the United States, the Soviet Union and South Africa and was everywhere fêted as a great man. His fame was not due solely to his plays but to the public image he had created for himself as a controversialist, ready to give his views – often challenging and deliberately provocative – on all manner of subjects. He was invariably amusing and stimulating, but sometimes extravagant and outrageous in what he said and wrote. As the introduction to the Penguin edition of *Pygmalion* says, 'Essentially shy, he yet created the persona of G.B.S., the showman, satirist, controversialist, critic, pundit, wit, intellectual buffoon and dramatist.'

Shaw developed his ideas of Socialism over a long period and his views were much different from those of most socialists today. However, his hatred of inequality and class exploitation never faded. He also developed a personal philosophy, expressed in *Man and Superman*, whereby he saw the future of the human race as depending on gradually evolving a higher kind of human being – a superman, in fact.

Shaw died in 1950 at the age of ninety-four. His death brought tributes from all over the world to honour the man who for more than half a century had entertained, teased, infuriated and delighted his audiences and readers – and, above all, had made them think hard about things they usually took for granted.

## BACKGROUND TO *PYGMALION*

The idea from which *Pygmalion* developed came to Shaw as early as 1897, thirteen years before he actually wrote the play. He had been to the theatre to see the great actor, Forbes Robertson, play Hamlet to Mrs Patrick Campbell's Ophelia. All thoughts were driven from his head, he said, 'by a play I want to write for them, in which he shall be a west end gentleman and she an east end dona in an apron and three orange and red ostrich feathers'. But he did nothing with this germ of an idea until in 1912 the actor-manager, George Alexander, asked him to write a play for his theatre. Shaw agreed and went away and wrote *Pygmalion*.

Shaw had promised the part of Eliza to Mrs Patrick Campbell, but George Alexander refused to work with this temperamental star; consequently there were delays and disputes over casting and management before a date could be fixed and a theatre found for the English première. All this took two years and in the meantime the play had been translated into German and already performed with great success in Germany and Austria. Its much-heralded first performance in London took place on 11 April 1914 at His Majesty's Theatre.

Rehearsals had been anything but smooth. Shaw directed the production himself but had the greatest difficulty in persuading his leading actors to portray the characters as he wished. The part of Professor Higgins was taken by Herbert Beerbohm Tree (later Sir Herbert Tree), the last of the great Victorian actor-managers. He was accustomed to playing classical roles and romantic heroes and he found himself at a loss with the unusual character of Higgins. Shaw once said of him, 'He tried hard . . . and when he resigned himself to his unnatural task, he set to work to make this disagreeable and incredible person sympathetic in the character of a lover, for which I left so little room that he was quite baffled . . .' More than twenty years later, Beerbohm Tree's grandson, the actor David Tree, auditioned for and got the part of Freddy in the film of the play. Shaw accepted him with the words, 'After all, you could scarcely make a greater mess of it than your grandfather made of Higgins.'

Mrs Patrick Campbell was even more difficult. She found Eliza's cockney speech impossible and such quarrels broke out between Shaw and his tempestuous leading lady that in the end she refused to rehearse with him in the theatre. Shaw eventually produced the play by means of letters of instructions sent via the assistant stage manager!

Despite these setbacks, the opening night was a tremendous success, Mrs Campbell scoring a great hit. The 'Not bloody likely' remark from Act Three was greeted by a shocked gasp from the audience and this was followed by such a gale of laughter that the play almost came to a halt.

From the very first performance of *Pygmalion*, Shaw suffered from actors who wanted to force a romantic ending despite his lines. Shaw had left very little time for anything between the closing lines of the play and the fall of the curtain. Even so, Beerbohm Tree managed to grab flowers and throw them with romantic ardour towards Eliza as she left the stage. Shaw, who had been delighted with the success of his play up to this point, was so furious that he left the theatre, refusing to congratulate the cast, meet the press or attend the first-night party. Instead, he went home alone and read Shakespeare in bed for an hour before going to sleep!

Since that first night, *Pygmalion* has held its place as one of Shaw's most popular plays with the public. It reached large audiences in a film version made in 1938 and more recently was adapted as the musical comedy, *My Fair Lady* by Alan Jay Lerner with music by Frederick Loewe. This, too, was made into a film, with Rex Harrison as Higgins and Audrey Hepburn as Eliza.


## Note on the Film Insertions

The Penguin edition of *Pygmalion* includes scenes from the script of the 1938 film of the play, together with linking narrative. Shaw himself says in his Note for Technicians (page 11), 'For ordinary theatrical use the scenes separated by rows of asterisks are to be omitted.' Accordingly in this book these scenes are not included in the Synopsis and Act by Act Analysis. They are, however, discussed in a special section entitled 'Scenes from the Film' on pp. 45–9.

# Synopsis of the Play

## ACT ONE

A varied group of people are sheltering from the rain under the portico of St Paul's church, Covent Garden. It is 11.15 p.m. and the theatres have just closed. Among those present are a mother and daughter, both in evening dress, a number of bystanders and a man who, with his back turned to the others, is busily writing in a notebook.

The daughter is irritated that her brother Freddy has not been able to find a taxi and her mother shares her feelings. Their mood is not improved when one of the bystanders remarks that there will not be any cabs available for a quarter of an hour. His opinion is borne out by Freddy himself who dashes in to say there are no taxis anywhere. His mother and sister badger him into going out in the rain to try once more.

Just as he rushes off, he bumps into a flower girl who is coming in from the rainy street, knocking her basket from her hands and scattering her flowers. He does not stay to help her pick them up, despite her cry, 'Nah then, Freddy: look wh'y' gowin, deah'.

The flower girl is a dirty, unkempt creature but the mother approaches her to ask how she knows her son's name. The girl's explanation is simple: she simply chanced on that name as a casual form of address. The mother gives the girl sixpence in recompense for the scattering of her flowers.

An elderly gentleman of military bearing joins the group and, not wishing to buy a flower from the girl, gives her some coins to keep her quiet. An interfering bystander warns her that another man is taking down all she is saying in a notebook. The girl is very alarmed, particularly at the suggestion that the man is a police informer taking evidence that she is begging. She demands to see what is in the notebook but finds it impossible to understand. The note taker, however, reads it back to her, reproducing her cockney accent exactly. He then proceeds to tell people in the crowd where they live, correctly placing the girl as being from Lisson Grove. He delights his audience by accurately placing the elderly gentleman also.

The daughter comes forward to express her impatience at her brother's failure to return with a taxi and she is not pleased when the note taker correctly places her and her mother. He then points out that the rain has stopped and the crowd disperses, leaving only the flower girl, the gentleman and the note taker.

The gentleman asks the note taker how he can place people with such assurance. He explains that he does it through the science of speech. He talks of his skill in training people to learn a new speech in order to disguise their humble origins. During this conversation the flower girl has been grumbling and complaining about the way the note taker has treated her. When he turns and rebukes her so crushingly that she utters a long drawn-out wail, he notes down the horrid sound, telling the gentleman that in three months he could train the girl to speak in such a way that she would be accepted as a duchess at an ambassador's garden party.

The men now introduce themselves to each other. The note taker is Professor Henry Higgins, an expert in speech, and the gentleman is a retired soldier, Colonel Pickering, a student of Indian dialects. Since both have long wanted to meet, they are delighted to make each other's acquaintance at last. They decide to have supper together. As they leave, the flower girl tries again to sell Pickering a flower, saying she is short of money for her lodging. But Higgins remembers that she had previously spoken of having some change and calls her a liar. Angrily the girl throws the whole basket of flowers at his feet 'for sixpence'. The chimes of the church clock remind him of his duty to be charitable. He therefore flings a whole handful of money into her basket and goes off with Pickering.

As the flower girl excitedly counts the money, Freddy returns looking for his mother and sister. He is dismayed to learn that they have already left, but the flower girl, intoxicated by such wealth, hires a taxi herself, grandly telling the driver to take her to Buckingham Palace. She explains to him that she does not want Freddy to hear her real but humble address – Angel Court, Drury Lane.

## ACT TWO

The next morning at his home in Wimpole Street, Higgins is showing his speech laboratory to Colonel Pickering when he is told that a young girl has called to see him. It is the flower girl; her name is Eliza Doolittle. She tells the men that she has come to take speech lessons so that she can work as a lady in a flower shop. She is prepared to pay a shilling per lesson. The men are both amused and amazed at her. Higgins works out that she is offering a huge proportion of her very small income and declares it to be the biggest offer he has ever received. The girl is alarmed and confused by this talk and by the harsh way Higgins speaks to her.

However, Colonel Pickering's interest has been aroused. He challenges Higgins to a wager: if he can indeed, as claimed, pass the girl off as a duchess at an ambassador's party, he will hail him as the greatest teacher alive – and pay all the expenses of the experiment and of the lessons as well. Higgins accepts the bet. He sends the girl off with his housekeeper, Mrs Pearce, to be bathed and given new clothes. He brushes aside all questions about the girl's position in the house, despite pleas from Colonel Pickering and Mrs Pearce for him to be sensible. His talk is so unreasonable and his treatment of Eliza so unfeeling that the girl rushes for the door. But, unwilling to lose this opportunity to prove his skill, Higgins waylays her and promises her chocolates, taxis and riches if she stays. Pickering insists that he explain to the girl exactly what she is undertaking. Higgins does this in his own way and Mrs Pearce says that she will speak to the girl in private. Eliza reluctantly agrees to stay and, still complaining bitterly, is led off by Mrs Pearce.

Pickering gains an assurance from Higgins that no advantage will be taken of Eliza while she is in the house. Mrs Pearce returns and points out very firmly that neither Higgins's swearing nor his table manners will be a good example to the girl.

A dustman named Alfred Doolittle is then announced. He turns out to be Eliza's father and at once demands the return of his daughter. To his surprise and dismay, Higgins immediately agrees. Having learned by chance that his daughter is staying at Higgins's house – and has sent for her clothes and belongings – Doolittle has come along to scrounge some money. Higgins suggests he is trying to blackmail him, but Doolittle denies this and asks for a chance to explain. He is prepared to allow his daughter to stay for five pounds; if he thought Higgins's intentions were dishonourable he would ask fifty! He sets out his philosophy of life: he is one of the undeserving poor and, although he enjoys the freedom and happiness this brings, he is resentful that he is opposed by middle-class morality, which he sees as just an excuse for never giving him anything.

Much amused, Higgins offers him ten pounds, but Doolittle will take only five. As he is about to leave the room, he politely stands aside to admit a dainty Japanese lady. He fails to recognize Eliza, fresh from her bath and wearing a kimono. Everyone is amazed at the transformation. Eliza has enjoyed the bathroom with its scented soap and soft towels, but was forced by her sense of decency to cover the mirror with a towel before she bathed. Higgins ironically remarks that Doolittle has brought up his daughter too strictly, to which the dustman replies that a lick of the strap was his only contribution. As Doolittle leaves, Higgins makes sure he will not come back by telling him he should visit his daughter regularly and that next time a clergyman will be available to help him in his talks with her. Doolittle departs hastily. An announcement that the new clothes have arrived sends Eliza from the room, shrieking with excitement. The men agree that they have taken on a stiff job.

## ACT THREE

It is some months later. Higgins calls on his mother to tell her that he has invited a flower girl whom he has been training to visit her that afternoon. Mrs Higgins is dismayed at the prospect but explanations are interrupted by the arrival of Mrs Eynsford Hill, her daughter, Clara, and her son, Freddy. Shortly afterwards they are joined by Colonel Pickering. There is an awkward conversation, marked by Higgins's rudeness, as they wait for Eliza.

When Eliza does arrive, her beauty, her air of distinction and her fashionable clothes create a sensation. Freddy is immediately infatuated with her. Higgins is not at all pleased to realize that the

Eynsford Hills are the same family who sheltered under the portico of St Paul's church on that first evening.

Mrs Higgins opens the conversation by talking about the weather; Eliza responds in a highly stilted manner, to the great amusement of Freddy. Talk of influenza leads her to unexpected family reminiscences about an aunt who was supposed to have died of 'flu but was quite probably murdered by those who wanted to steal her hat! This of course astonishes Mrs Eynsford Hill, who is further alarmed by Eliza's views on gin drinking. To cover up the outrageous tone of Eliza's conversation in such polite company, Higgins explains that she is using the new, fashionable small talk. Eliza feels she is being a great success and is cross with Freddy for laughing at her, but he explains that he is really enjoying the new small talk. Relieved, Eliza is about to say more when Higgins signals for her to leave. She obediently rises, says her farewells with perfect elocution, but devastates everyone present by replying to Freddy's offer to walk with her across the park with, 'Walk! Not bloody likely. I am going in a taxi'.

Quite taken aback by all this, Mrs Eynsford Hill takes her leave. As they go, Higgins encourages the impressionable Clara to try the new small talk at the next at-home they attend. Freddy is delighted to be invited by Mrs Higgins to call again when Eliza is present.

Higgins and Colonel Pickering are anxious for Mrs Higgins's reaction to Eliza. She tells them frankly that the girl's conversation gives her away at once. She then questions her son about Eliza's position in his household. Higgins refuses to answer this directly, but he and Pickering chat enthusiastically about how interesting they find their work with Eliza. Mrs Higgins quietens them and confronts them with the problem of Eliza's future, but both men prefer to ignore this beyond answering that something will be found for her. They leave to take Eliza to an exhibition. The frustrated Mrs Higgins exclaims, 'Oh men! men!! men!!!'

## ACT FOUR

After further training Eliza is successfully passed off as a duchess and Higgins wins his bet with Pickering. The three of them return home after this night of triumph but their mood is subdued. The men are tired: Higgins thanks God it is all over and declares that the whole thing has been a bore. Eliza's expression is almost tragic as the men completely ignore her, even when she fetches Higgins's slippers for him. Tired out after her ordeal and entirely neglected by the men, her nerves are near breaking point. The men go to bed without even saying goodnight to her. Left alone, she gives way to feelings of anger and frustration and flings herself to the floor. When Higgins unexpectedly returns to look for his slippers, Eliza throws them at him. She vents her fury on him and even tries to scratch his face, so upset is she about his neglect of her feelings and so worried about the future.

In the tense calm that follows this outburst, Higgins asks if anyone has offended or ill-treated her. Eliza is too crushed to offer much response, except a heart-felt cry, 'Oh God! I wish I was dead'. Higgins seems incapable of understanding her and patronizingly tells her to have a little cry and say her prayers before going to bed. But Eliza passionately asks what she is now good for, where she is to go and what is to become of her. Higgins treats this very casually, suggesting that she will easily settle into some way of life. She might even marry; perhaps his mother could find a husband for her. Eliza sees this as selling herself, though Higgins disagrees, saying she can refuse a proposal if she so wishes. He suggests that perhaps Pickering could set her up in a florist's shop. This reminds Higgins that Pickering must pay several bills for Eliza's clothes and the hire of her jewellery. Eliza, addressing him as 'sir' and adopting the tone of a servant, demands to know if the clothes belong to her or the colonel, as she does not want to be accused of stealing if she takes them away. Eliza's attitude shocks and angers Higgins, much to her delight since she has at last succeeded in arousing genuine emotion in him. He tells her to take 'the whole damned houseful' if she likes, except for the jewels, which are hired. Eliza remembers that one ring was a gift to her from Higgins. She hands this back to him with the others, saying that she no longer wants it. He hurls it furiously into the fireplace and turns as if to hit her. He denies this intention, claiming it is she who has struck him to the heart. Again Eliza is delighted to have got a little of her own back. Higgins attempts to leave the room with great dignity, cursing her and his own folly in wasting his time on 'a heartless

guttersnipe', but ruins the effect by slamming the door as he goes.
Eliza looks for the ring on the hearth and finds it, only to fling it
down on to the dessert stand before going upstairs 'in a tearing rage'.
She intends to leave the house.

## ACT FIVE

Full of concern about Eliza's departure, Higgins and Pickering visit
Mrs Higgins, not knowing that Eliza has already sought refuge with
her. Their conversation is interrupted by the arrival of Alfred Doolittle, now transformed into a gentleman and dressed for a fashionable
wedding. He is very upset about his change of status and blames
Higgins for destroying his happiness by recommending him to an
American millionaire as the most original moralist in England. As a
result, the millionaire has left him a fortune. Doolittle cannot bring
himself to refuse the money as he fears ending his days in the
workhouse, but he sees himself now as a victim of middle-class
morality, under pressure of which he is about to marry Eliza's 'step-
mother'.

Mrs Higgins reveals that Eliza is in the house. She asks Doolittle to
wait on the balcony until Eliza has made it up with the two men. Eliza
joins them and talks with great self-possession to Pickering. She
thanks him for all he has taught her by his example and dismisses
Higgins's contribution by saying that he had merely done his job as a
speech teacher. Higgins is very angry at her superior attitude and
declares that she will relapse 'into the gutter in three weeks' without
him at her elbow. But Eliza is confident that she could never utter
one of her old sounds if she tried. The sudden appearance of her
father, however, dressed in all his finery, so startles her that she
utters her old cry of 'A-a-a-a-a-ah-ow-ooh'. Higgins is jubilant: he feels
his point has been proved.

Doolittle asks Eliza, Mrs Higgins and Pickering to attend his
wedding. They agree and Mrs Higgins goes to get ready. As Pickering
leaves with Doolittle, he asks Eliza to stay on with them at Wimpole
Street.

Left alone together, Eliza and Higgins at last confront the problem of her future. Higgins yields nothing: if she comes back, he will not change his manners in any way. He believes in treating everyone the same. Eliza insists she will not be passed over. Higgins will not concede anything, even on this point, but he does say he has become accustomed to her and will miss her if she goes. Eliza sees this as an example of his skill in twisting a girl's heart when he does not care for her at all. He replies that he cares for life and he will not trade in affection. If she comes back, it must be for the sake of good fellowship and each can be free to break the arrangement at any time. But Eliza is not free. She has lost her independence. When Higgins considers the possibility of arranging a marriage for her, she firmly rejects the idea, but reveals that Freddy Eynsford Hill is very much in love with her. Higgins is extremely angry at this and asks if she wants him to be equally infatuated with her. Eliza denies this; what she wants is a little kindness and human feeling. Higgins scornfully lectures her on the contrast between his cold but intellectually satisfying way of life and what he calls 'the life of the gutter' with its warmth and violence. He tells her to go back to it if that is what she wants.

Eliza is deeply upset by this cruel speech because Higgins must know that she cannot revert to her old life. She declares that, since Freddy loves her, she will marry him as soon as she can support him. Suddenly she realizes how she can gain the freedom she needs: she will become a teacher, using Higgins's methods to train others as she has been trained. At first Higgins is furious, but then his anger dissolves into wonder as he realizes that he has indeed created a woman in the full sense of the word – a really independent person, able to survive without him.

Mrs Higgins returns, ready for Doolittle's wedding. When she gently hints at the possibility of marriage between Eliza and either her son or Colonel Pickering, Higgins laughs uproariously, declaring she is going to marry Freddy.

# Act by Act Analysis

## ACT ONE

The play begins late at night in the heart of London's theatreland. It is pouring with rain and all sorts of people are sheltering under the portico of St Paul's church, Covent Garden, formerly the site of the famous fruit and vegetable market. In this unlikely setting, we are introduced to several of the main characters of the play.

A mother and daughter, whom we later learn to be Mrs Eynsford Hill and Clara, are waiting impatiently for a cab which Clara's brother, Freddy, has gone to look for. The girl is irritable, the mother more resigned, but when Freddy returns without a taxi both women turn on him angrily and insist that he try again.

Even in this brief episode it is clear that Clara dominates her mother and expects her own way, while Freddy is well meaning but ineffective.

As Freddy leaves, he bumps into a flower girl who is hurrying in out of the rain and he knocks her basket from her hands. 'Nah then, Freddy: look wh'y' gowin, deah,' she cries. This is Eliza Doolittle, a typical London flower girl of the period. She is poorly dressed in an old straw hat, shabby coat and skirt with a rough apron – and she is very dirty.

She sits at the foot of a pillar and grumbles in a broad cockney accent as she picks up the scattered flowers. But Mrs Eynsford Hill is intrigued because the girl has addressed her son as Freddy. She asks how she knows her son's name. The girl replies that she doesn't: 'Freddy' might have been 'Charlie', a mere pleasantry to make a stranger feel at ease.

Another important character in the play now makes his entrance: he is Colonel Pickering, called at this point simply 'The Gentleman'. When he stands near Eliza, she tries to sell him a flower. He has no small change except three halfpence, which he gives her and she accepts this as being better than nothing.

At this point the play explodes into action. A busy-body of a bystander, knowing that begging is an offence, warns Eliza to give the gentleman a flower for his money because there is a man with a notebook taking down her every word! Eliza is terrified that the man is a police informer and she makes a tremendous scene protesting her innocence and respectability, while the bystanders join in with advice, warnings and cries of support for her. She appeals to the gentleman for help, but the noise is cut short when the 'note taker' steps forward. He denies that he is a policeman but Eliza insists on seeing what he has written about her. The writing is in a code she cannot understand. 'That aint proper writing. I cant read that,' she complains. It is, of course, phonetic script, which reproduces the actual sound of the speaker's words. When he reads out Eliza's words in her own cockney accent, she is still convinced he is a policeman.

In the hubbub that follows, the note taker calmly identifies the flower girl's place of origin and the bystanders by their accents. They, much offended, challenge him to identify the background of the gentleman. The note taker correctly places the colonel's background as Cheltenham, Harrow, Cambridge and India.

Growing impatient with all this, Clara Eynsford Hill pushes forward to ask what Freddy can be doing all this time. This brings her and her mother to the attention of the note taker, who correctly places their origins also, much to the annoyance of Clara, though her mother is impressed. Realizing that they want a cab, the note taker blows a blast on a whistle, recognized by a bystander as a sporting rather than a police whistle. The note taker quietly remarks that the rain has stopped and the group disperses. As they do so, a sarcastic bystander suggests that the note taker himself is from the Hanwell lunatic asylum. The Eynsford Hills go off to find a bus.

Many things have already been established. There are very clear class distinctions – the bystanders and the flower girl know themselves to be very different from the gentleman and from the mother and daughter. They are less sure about the note taker, who remains a mysterious figure. His ability to identify their origins so readily disturbs them and they are glad to get away from him. More will be revealed about this man in the next part of the act. Up to now he strikes us as self assured, careless of his effect on other people and confidently superior in his dealings with Eliza and the bystanders.

The flower girl is endowed with cockney cheerfulness and a readiness to be friendly with anybody. She is excitable in her reactions and prone to self-pity when things go wrong for her. These qualities will be developed and transformed as the play goes on. The cheeriness will develop into a spirited determination to succeed at whatever cost; her natural friendliness will enable her to win sympathy and support in the new circle in which she will move, and in Act Four the self-pity will be replaced by a profound questioning of her role in society and her ability to survive as a really independent woman. The play is about the transformation of Eliza and she begins this transformation in Covent Garden. She is far from being the 'squashed cabbage leaf' the note taker describes her as. She is fully alive, a real human being and full of character. But she is oppressed by her poverty, her lack of education and her cockney speech. The society of the period offers her no obvious way of escape.

When the other people leave the shelter of the church, only the note taker, Colonel Pickering and Eliza remain. The two men try to ignore her but her continued complaints irritate the note taker whose eloquent rebuke amazes Eliza so much that she utters her famous cry, 'Ah-ah-ah-ow-ow-ow-oo'. This draws from the note taker the boast from which the whole plot develops. He declares the girl's 'kerbstone English' will keep her in the gutter all her life. 'Well, sir, in three months I could pass that girl off as a duchess at an ambassador's garden party,' he says.

Eliza is immediately interested but the men turn to their own conversation. The note taker introduces himself as Professor Higgins, an expert in English speech. Colonel Pickering is a student of Indian dialects who has come from India especially to meet Higgins. The two men decide to sup together. As they leave, Eliza tries to sell Pickering a flower, pleading that she has not enough money for her lodgings. Higgins remembers how she had previously offered change for half-a-crown to Pickering and calls her a liar. Her quick temper flares and she throws the whole basket at his feet 'for sixpence'. The chimes of the church clock remind him to be charitable and he flings a handful of coins into her basket as he leaves with Pickering.

As the delighted Eliza counts her sudden wealth, Freddy comes back with a taxi only to find his mother and sister have left. Eliza solves his problem for him: 'Never mind, young man. I'm going home in a taxi,' she says triumphantly and sails off.

By the end of this act, the identity of Professor Higgins is fully revealed. We see in the way he speaks to Eliza his total insensitivity to other people's feelings. He calls her a squashed cabbage leaf, a disgrace to the noble architecture of the columns of the church and so on – and then ignores her completely. When he finally gives her money, it is thrown casually into her basket. He is utterly self absorbed.

Eliza's reactions at the end of the scene are a foretaste of things to come. Her sudden impulse to ride in a taxi and her reluctance to reveal to Freddy the poor district in which she lives show her hidden dream of bettering herself in the world. She makes what she considers to be a stylish exit and she is therefore much offended when the taximan suggests she has probably never been in a taxi before.

## ACT TWO

The next day Colonel Pickering is with Higgins in his laboratory in Wimpole Street when Mrs Pearce, the housekeeper, announces that a young woman has called to see the professor. Mrs Pearce clearly disapproves of this very common girl but thinks the Professor might be interested in her accent. Higgins agrees and the girl is brought in. It is Eliza, outrageously dressed in what she considers her finery. Higgins needs only one glance to recognize the flower girl and rudely dismisses her, saying he already has recordings of her Lisson Grove speech. But Eliza, having courageously made her way to the Professor's house, is not to be put off so easily. To the amazement of Higgins and Pickering, she reveals the purpose of her visit: she wants Higgins to teach her to speak properly so that she can be a lady in a flower shop. What is more, she is ready to pay for lessons. She has worked out that since a friend of hers has lessons in French for eighteen pence an hour, the reasonable fee for learning her own language would be a shilling (five pence). Higgins realizes that this is two-fifths of her daily income and quickly proves that her shilling is the equivalent of sixty pounds for a millionaire. He declares it to be the biggest offer he has ever had! Believing that the lessons must be sixty pounds each, Eliza bursts into tears – to be threatened with a broomstick by Higgins if she does not stop snivelling.

The comedy so far arises from Eliza's ill-conceived attempts to lend dignity to her appearance, her bearing and her efforts to negotiate on equal terms with Higgins, although she is hopelessly ignorant of the way to go about it. We are amused too by Higgins's brusqueness to her and his unexpected assessment of the fee she is offering. At the same time, we sympathize with Eliza and are less impressed with the way Higgins and Pickering joke about her name, and Higgins's casual disregard of her as a person. However, the courtesy of Colonel Pickering is already in evidence when he gently asks her what she wants (p. 38) and politely offers her a chair (p. 39).

Pickering now sets the whole plot in motion when he says, 'Higgins, I'm interested. What about the ambassador's garden party?' (p. 40). He offers to pay for the lessons and wagers Higgins all his expenses if he can succeed in transforming Eliza. Higgins at once accepts the challenge: 'I shall make a duchess of the draggletailed guttersnipe' (p. 41). He decides to start work immediately and orders Eliza to be scrubbed and dressed in new clothes. If she gives any trouble, she is to be walloped and if there is no room for her in the house she can be put in the dustbin.

Everyone protests at this extravagant unreasonableness, but Higgins, in a sudden change of mood, disclaims any intention of being unkind or overbearing – much to the amusement of Pickering. Mrs Pearce then has a chance to make her point: '. . . you cant take a girl up like that as if you were picking up a pebble on a beach' (p. 42). But Higgins quickly elicits from Eliza that she is unmarried and has been turned out by her parents to fend for herself. He therefore sees no obstacle to his plan and airily tells Mrs Pearce that she can adopt the girl as her daughter. But the housekeeper tries to pin him down to such practical details as to the girl's pay and – the important question – what is to become of her. Higgins absolutely refuses to be bothered by any such details, callously remarking, 'when I've done with her, we can throw her back in the gutter'. No wonder Eliza replies, 'Oh, youve no feeling heart in you: you dont care for nothing but yourself'.

But Higgins does not want to lose the subject of his experiment so quickly. He intercepts Eliza, pops half a chocolate cream in her mouth (the other half he eats himself to re-assure her that he has not drugged it) and then promises her a future filled with chocolates, taxis, gold and diamonds and an officer in the Guards for a husband (p. 45).

Pickering now intervenes in support of Mrs Pearce. The girl must understand quite clearly what she is doing if she consents to be a pupil for six months. Higgins replies scornfully that Eliza is incapable of understanding anything. She simply needs to be given her orders. He sets these out, reasonably enough at first, but then comes out with the extravagant threat that the King will have her head cut off if he finds out she is not really a lady. Mrs Pearce undertakes to explain matters more sensibly and takes her off to the bathroom. Eliza is completely bewildered, very frightened and goes out protesting that she has always been a good girl, won't be 'put upon' and has feelings the same as anyone else . . .

For all our interest in Eliza, it is Higgins who dominates the stage in this section (pp. 40–45). From the moment Pickering challenges him to transform Eliza into a duchess, he is completely taken up with the idea. He must begin at once, pausing only for Eliza to be cleaned by Mrs Pearce. Eliza is of no importance to him whatsoever except as a sporting challenge to his skill as a teacher. The fact that she is 'deliciously low' only makes the task more exciting. He seems not to care a jot that Eliza might resent being called 'low' or 'a guttersnipe' or being consigned to a dustbin. The only thing that matters is what he can train her to do. Of course, his high-handed behaviour and Eliza's protests are the source of great amusement to the audience and Shaw gains more comedy from Higgins's elaborate denial that he wishes to give offence: 'I never had the slightest intention of walking over anyone. All I propose is that we should be kind to this poor girl . . .' (p. 42).

Higgins is clearly enjoying himself in this scene, for he consciously uses his skill as a speaker to dominate Eliza, not only in the speech mentioned above, but also when he promises Eliza that 'the streets will be strewn with the bodies of men shooting themselves' for her sake (p. 42), and in the long speech (pp. 45 and 46) when he sets out Eliza's 'orders'. He is certainly taking an unfair advantage of Eliza's lack of education and gives her every reason to exclaim, 'Oh, youve no feeling heart in you: you dont care for nothing but yourself'.

Colonel Pickering and Mrs Pearce do what they can to induce Higgins to discuss the affair reasonably but he cannot be bothered with petty details. It is as well that Mrs Pearce undertakes to 'speak to the girl properly in private' as she bundles her off to the bath. Eliza's protests as she leaves the room are a pathetic attempt to re-assert her own lost dignity.

As the act continues, Higgins explains to Pickering his desire to remain a confirmed old bachelor. He assures the Colonel that he has no dishonourable intentions where Eliza is concerned. She will be a pupil and, as such, sacred. Then follows a passage of light comedy in which Higgins has to submit to Mrs Pearce's criticisms of his language and his table manners which, she says, will be a bad influence on the girl if he persists in them. For once Higgins is at a disadvantage and Pickering is much amused to see him on the defensive.

Shaw now introduces a new and striking character into the play. So far Eliza has been the only lower-class character to invade this comfortable middle-class world; but she is about to be joined, most unexpectedly, by her dustman father, Alfred Doolittle. His appearance is startling for he is in his working clothes. He says he has come to demand the return of his daughter. Higgins (who cannot resist placing him by his accent from Hounslow, mother probably Welsh) takes the wind out of his sails by replying briskly, 'Of course you do . . . Take her away at once' (p. 53). Doolittle of course wants to get some money out of Higgins and the reply is not at all what he wants. Higgins, thoroughly in control of the situation, accuses him of sending his daughter on purpose as an excuse for blackmail and pretends he is about to phone the police. But Doolittle points out that he has never mentioned money, even though everyone realizes his motive. Higgins is still suspicious. Doolittle says he has not seen his daughter for two months; how therefore does he know where she is?

Doolittle explains that he met the boy whom Eliza had sent back to her lodgings to collect her belongings and decided to bring them over himself. Any pretence of his coming to rescue his daughter is destroyed by Higgins's question, 'But why did you bring her luggage if you intended to take her away?' Obviously rescue was not really his intention. Higgins sends for Mrs Pearce to bring Eliza and give her to her father. But she has no clothes (her old ones having been burnt) and must wait for new ones. This enables Doolittle to put his case to the gentlemen as between 'men of the world'.

He suggests that five pounds would be a reasonable sum to pay him to satisfy his rights as a father. If Higgins's motives were improper, he would ask fifty pounds! Pickering is shocked. He asks, 'Have you no morals, man?' 'Cant afford them, Governor,' replies Doolittle (p. 58). He then launches into his famous case against middle-class morality, for he has chosen to be one of the undeserving poor.

As Doolittle sees it, there are two kinds of poor people – the deserving and the undeserving. These labels are attached to them by the middle class, who will only give charity to those they consider respectable and respectful. Such poor people must at least give the impression of living decent and sober lives, even though they may in reality be less honest than they appear. These are the deserving poor. Doolittle is too vigorous and independent to lower himself to gain charity in this way. He prefers to be undeserving, going his own way and enjoying life as he can. All the same, he resents the fact that this keeps him from the assistance the so-called deserving poor can receive. He blames middle-class morality which he sees as just an excuse for never giving him anything. Yet he likes being undeserving and intends to go on that way. He ends by asking five pounds for his daughter.

Higgins is greatly impressed by the dustman's natural eloquence and his frank acceptance of his undeserving way of life. He even offers him ten pounds, but such wealth would be too much for Doolittle; it might make him careful and money-conscious. He refuses to take more than five, which he says will be just enough for a week-end spree with his missus.

He takes the money and is anxious to leave. On his way out he pauses in the doorway to allow a charming young Japanese lady to enter the room. He does not recognize Eliza, now bathed and dressed in some clothes Higgins had brought home from the East. Everyone is amazed at the change in Eliza's appearance. When she puts on her feathered hat, it seems to Higgins that she has successfully created a new fashion. Although pleased with her appearance and the comforts of the bathroom, Eliza has been shocked at finding a mirror there in which she could see her unclothed body. Eliza is determined to remain a good girl and Higgins's threat that if she says that again she will be sent home with her father has no effect on her. She knows he has only come for money. This declaration angers Doolittle and his mood is not helped when Eliza puts out her tongue at him. Pickering has to keep them apart and Doolittle, now that he has had his money, is ready to go. When he has left, Eliza thinks she would like to go in a taxi to show off to her former friends in Tottenham Court Road, but decides to wait until she has some fashionable clothes. Mrs Pearce's announcement that new clothes have arrived sends Eliza rushing off to see them, uttering her cry of 'Ah-ow-oo-ooh!' Higgins and Pickering agree they have taken on a stiff task.

Doolittle's arrival promises complications in the plot which do not, in fact, develop. Shaw makes it clear that Doolittle, having got his money, wants nothing more to do with Eliza and will in no way interfere with Higgins's lessons. He appears only once more in the play (Act Five), when his transformation into the caricature of a gentleman makes him a victim of the middle-class morality he so vigorously denounces in this scene. His eloquent speech (p. 58) and his whole attitude challenge the comfortable acceptance of the code of behaviour that all the other characters see as normal – and moral. It will be Doolittle's unhappy fate to be taken up and patronized as an amusing eccentric by the very people he so strongly resents.

## ACT THREE

Act Three opens with Mrs Higgins's 'at-home' day, on which her friends may call upon her. She is, however, not at all happy to see her unsociable son, but Higgins explains why he is here. He has for some months been training a flower girl to speak and behave properly. The girl is getting on well and Higgins expects to win his bet with Pickering that he will successfully pass her off as a duchess in six months. Although he does not have time to explain fully, he seems to think that his mother's 'at-home' – to which he has invited the girl – will be a useful first step into society for Eliza. He has told her to limit her conversation to the weather and people's health.

In this opening section we see how very fond of his mother Higgins is, so much so that he says he cannot be bothered with younger women. His ideal woman is someone just like his mother. Mrs Higgins comments on his manners from time to time and treats him as a small boy, though with great delicacy and politeness. Higgins is confident that he has trained Eliza sufficiently for her to avoid making social gaffes, but Mrs Higgins is less certain. She sees the danger of the girl discussing people's health!

They are interrupted by the arrival of Mrs Eynsford Hill and Clara. Higgins runs true to form as he brusquely replies to their conversational pleasantries. Colonel Pickering joins the party, as does Freddy, thus completing the group of people ready to greet Eliza's appearance. The problem is what to talk about. As Higgins says, 'Well, here we are, anyhow! And now what the devil are we going to talk about until Eliza comes?' (p. 72). Clara's suggestion that people should always talk frankly prompts Higgins to denounce the general ignorance of people – including those present. Mrs Higgins gently refers to an ignorance of manners, which her son is just now displaying.

Eliza's entry is stunning. Her beauty and her elegant clothes make such an impression on the company that they all rise to greet her. Eliza, guided by Higgins's signals, successfully goes through the motions of the introductions to Mrs Higgins and her guests. Higgins suddenly realizes that the Eynsford Hills are the family who sheltered from the rain in Covent Garden and in dismay he takes refuge on the divan after stumbling over the fire-irons en route.

After an awkward pause, Mrs Higgins tries to initiate a conversation by talking about the weather. Eliza startles the company by responding like a weather-forecaster. When Mrs Eynsford Hill refers to the possibility of cold weather bringing influenza, the flood gates of Eliza's eloquence are opened. Still enunciating her words beautifully, Eliza launches into the lurid details of an aunt who apparently died of influenza, though she suspects that her death had something to do with the theft of her new straw hat. The contrast between Eliza's voice and diction and her actual conversation bewilders the listeners, but Higgins covers up by declaring that Eliza is speaking the new small talk. Freddy is vastly amused, but Eliza takes great offence at his giggling: 'if I was doing it proper, what was you laughing at?' (p. 78). Mrs Higgins reassures her that she has not said anything she shouldn't and this encourages Eliza to go on. But Higgins feels she has said quite enough and signals for her to leave. Freddy, very taken with Eliza, offers to escort her across the park, but she rebuffs him with the devastating response: 'Not bloody likely. I am going in a taxi'. She leaves the room, unaware of the sensation she has caused.

The Eynsford Hills also leave, with Clara being wickedly encouraged by Higgins to use the new small talk at the other three at-homes she is to attend. Mrs Eynsford Hill is quite distressed by these new manners. She speaks pathetically to Mrs Higgins about the genteel poverty in which they live, with few parties for Clara, who really knows little of society. But she is pleased that Mrs Higgins likes Freddy and will always be glad to see him.

This scene is one of the classics of twentieth-century comedy. Such comedy arises from the incongruity of Eliza's voice and appearance on the one hand and the subject of her conversation on the other. She talks just as she would to the girls in Tottenham Court Road but in the accent of a well-born society lady. The audience enjoys the shock she is inflicting on the other guests and this pleasure is increased when Higgins encourages the Eynsford Hills to adopt the new small talk. Shaw cleverly paces the comedy – from the artificial greetings at Eliza's entrance to the increasingly hilarious domestic details of her family (especially the references to gin drinking) all delivered with such panache by Eliza, who really begins to enjoy herself as she grows more confident. Eliza's complete unawareness that she is saying anything untoward is a major element of the comic effect. The climax comes with her 'Not bloody likely'. The intrusion of what was considered in those days to be a really shocking swear word completes the disaster of Eliza's first excursion into society and provides the actress with one of the finest exit lines ever written!

When the visitors have left, Higgins and Pickering immediately ask Mrs Higgins what she thinks of Eliza. Is Eliza presentable? Quite rightly, Mrs Higgins tells them that she is far from ready – and her swearing is unlikely to be eliminated as long as she stays with Higgins! More seriously, Mrs Higgins questions the two men as to the terms on which Eliza is living at Wimpole Street. We learn from Higgins that Eliza is becoming useful to him, remembering his appointments and so on. His time is completely taken up with training her. Mrs Higgins considers them a pair of babies playing with a live doll. The men chatter enthusiastically about how quickly Eliza learns and Mrs Higgins has to quieten them down to ask the most vital question

Higgins has always avoided answering: what is to be done with Eliza afterwards? But the men are in no mood to bother with that question now. They rush off to take Eliza to an exhibition. Mrs Higgins tries to write a letter but gives it up and exclaims, understandably, 'Oh men! men!! men!!!'

Despite the relative failure of Eliza's appearance at Mrs Higgins's at-home, the possibility that she will be successful with further training is clear. At the end of this scene, Shaw again raises the really important question in the play: what is to happen to Eliza when Higgins has won his bet? The winning of the bet is no longer important in the play. We can take it for granted (even though the film-makers could not resist an extra scene in which we witness Eliza's triumph – see pp. 85–95). What matters now is Eliza's future and how much the newly acquired manner and speech of a duchess have made her a really independent woman. This question occupies us for the remainder of the play.

## ACT FOUR

It is midnight. The ambassador's party is over and Eliza has, predictably, triumphed. Higgins has won his bet and he, Pickering and Eliza return home, tired out. The voices of Higgins and Pickering are heard on the stairs, but Eliza enters first. There is no air of victory in this home-coming; the atmosphere is very much one of anti-climax. The great day has come and gone and the excitement of recent months is over. It is very much 'the morning after'.

In his stage directions Shaw describes Eliza's expression as 'almost tragic'. She sits brooding and silent as the men enter the room. They take no notice of her as they glance at the day's letters. Higgins declares the whole thing to have been a bore and he thanks God it is all over. He and Pickering totally ignore Eliza, even when she goes to fetch Higgins's slippers for him. They address no remark to her until Higgins tells her to put out the lights and tell Mrs Pearce that he will have tea, not coffee, in the morning. Neither of them actually bids her goodnight when they leave the room.

We may assume that Higgins and Pickering have treated Eliza like this all evening. They have shown no sensitivity to her feelings and neither praised nor thanked her for what she has done. When they return home, they do not bother to speak to her. Even the usually considerate Pickering has ignored her. This attitude creates Eliza's mood of tragic tension. She has been treated as a puppet with no will or feelings of her own. She has gone through the ordeal of winning Higgins's bet for him and then has been totally disregarded. What is more, she realizes that the experiment is over and she will have to face the future: she is too well spoken and well mannered to be a flower girl but has neither money of her own nor a certain place in middle-class society.

She has reached breaking point when Higgins returns to the room looking for his slippers. She snatches them up and throws them at him, telling him with great passion that she would like to smash his face and kill him. Quite overwrought, she screams and tries to tear her nails across his face. Higgins seizes her by the wrists and throws her into a chair, where she repeats, 'Whats to become of me? Whats to become of me?'

The usually self-confident Higgins is slightly shaken by this outburst and attempts, 'in his loftiest manner', to discover what is wrong. He asks Eliza if she has any cause for complaint over the way he or his household have behaved to her. When she denies this he tries to put her reaction down to tiredness and low spirits. But what rankles with Eliza is his remark, 'Thank God it's all over'. Higgins thinks that she too should be glad it is all over. He tells her she is free and can do what she likes. But Eliza is *not* free, and she knows it. Her training has rendered her fit for nothing. She has nowhere to go and nothing to do.

Brought face to face with her problem at last, Higgins still refuses to take it seriously. He says he had not realized she was going away. This remark catches the attention of both Eliza and the audience. Higgins makes nothing of it, but the suggestion that Eliza might continue to live with them as before is not lost on Eliza, although it is far from what she wants.

Higgins suggests that she might even marry, since she can be quite attractive. Not all men are confirmed bachelors like the colonel and himself. Eliza rejects this scornfully: she sees it as simply selling herself, though Higgins points out she can refuse a proposal if she dislikes it. He then suggests that Pickering has enough money to set her up in a florist's shop.

Throughout this conversation it is perfectly clear that Higgins pays no attention at all to Eliza's feelings. Obviously she cannot go back to being a flower girl, but he feels she can be disposed of in some way or other – marriage or some occupation that will not concern him. He persistently refuses to take Eliza seriously, precisely the sort of recognition that Eliza so badly wants. As far as this Pygmalion is concerned, Higgins has created the appearance of a duchess but he simply does not want to bother himself with her real personality.

Higgins continues to make insensitive remarks as he refers to all the money Pickering has spent on Eliza's clothing and jewellery. Eliza responds to this reference to her financial dependence on Pickering and Higgins by adopting the role of a menial. She surprises him by addressing him as 'sir' and asks whether her clothes belong to her or to Pickering, so that she will not be accused of stealing them if she takes them away. She insists that Higgins take over the jewels for the same reason. All this deeply offends Higgins, who accuses her of lacking feeling. But Eliza replies that she is only a common, ignorant girl and there cannot be any feelings between people of her class and his. All this makes Higgins very angry indeed but delights Eliza because, for the first time, she has managed to arouse some sort of feeling in him. He is not, for once, the cool, self-controlled Professor Higgins.

As Eliza gives the jewels to Higgins, she remembers a ring which he had once bought for her (no doubt very casually) in Brighton. She gives it to him, saying she no longer wants it. This is the last straw for Higgins. He flings the ring in the fireplace and seems to be about to hit her. He denies this intention but Eliza is thrilled that she has moved him to this extent. 'I'm glad. I've got a little of my own back, anyhow' (p. 104). She has reason to be satisfied. As he admits himself, she has made him lose his temper – something almost unknown to him. When Eliza pertly tells him to leave a note for Mrs Pearce, because she will not be passing on his message about his coffee in the morning, he solemnly damns Mrs Pearce, the coffee, Eliza and his own folly in lavishing his 'hard-earned knowledge and the treasure of . . . regard and intimacy on a heartless guttersnipe' (p. 105). He spoils his dignified exit and shows how hurt his feelings are by savagely slamming the door behind him.

Eliza searches in the fireplace for the ring, reluctant to lose the one token of Higgins's feelings for her. But when she finds it, she discards it again, flinging it on to the dessert stand as she goes upstairs 'in a tearing rage'.

Eliza's relationship with Higgins has in this act reached crisis level. Whatever Higgins might feel, things can never be the same again at Wimpole Street if Eliza returns. There is no sign she is anxious to do so. From the very beginning we have known that Eliza is a young woman with a will of her own and, as we have seen in Acts One and Two, not afraid to express her feelings. She has suppressed them as a willing pupil during her period of training, but now that is over the close relationship of teacher and pupil has also ended. All her resentment at his impersonal treatment of her during the last six months, and especially on her night of triumph, boils over, fuelled by the terror of finding herself adrift in the world with no occupation or place to go. Anger with him and at what has happened to her make her determined to leave at once.

Throughout this scene, Eliza demands emotional response, recognition that she is a woman. The cold intellectual world of Higgins does not satisfy her and Higgins will not change his ways for her or anyone. Eliza is thrilled that she has managed to provoke his anger, but it is a poor substitute for genuine, kind human feeling.

For Higgins, the experiment has proved a bore. He has shown his skill as a teacher but, in his own eyes, has achieved nothing significant. He seems to have forgotten his remark in Act Three about how interesting it is 'to take a human being and change her into a quite different human being by creating a new speech for her. It's filling up the deepest gulf that separates class from class and soul from soul' (pp. 81–2). There is no mention of this at the end of Act Four. The experiment is over and Higgins wants only to resume his intellectual pursuits and bachelor pleasures. But Eliza can neither go back to her former life nor, because she does not know how to, go forward. Furthermore, she totally rejects the cold life of the intellect which so appeals to Higgins. Her dilemma must be thrashed out and eventually resolved in Act Five.

## ACT FIVE

The last act of the play takes place in Mrs Higgins's drawing room. Shaw makes no secret of Eliza's presence: the audience is told in the first few lines that she is upstairs, having sought refuge with Mrs Higgins after her flight from Wimpole Street during the night.

Higgins and Pickering have been telephoning the police in their search for Eliza. Higgins bursts into his mother's room, very upset indeed. Mrs Higgins, knowing where Eliza is, remains completely calm but Higgins is 'in a state'. Typically, his concern is not for Eliza's safety but for the inconvenience caused to himself, because Eliza knows all his appointments and where he has put things. The conversation is interrupted by the announcement that a 'gentleman' called Mr Doolittle wants to see him urgently. Higgins thinks it must be some well-to-do relative to whom Eliza has gone for shelter. But the man who enters the room is Doolittle, the dustman – transformed into a society bridegroom in smart clothes, shining top hat with a flower in his button hole. It is a startling contrast with the ill-kempt dustman of Act Two.

Doolittle, however, is far from pleased with his new appearance. Without even noticing Mrs Higgins, he approaches her son and accuses him of being responsible for his change in circumstances and of thus ruining his happiness. Mrs Higgins greets him and, recovering his innate good manners, Doolittle apologizes for his outburst and sits down to recount his woes. It appears that Higgins had remarked in a letter to an American millionaire called Ezra D. Wannafeller that the most original moralist in England was one Alfred Doolittle, a common dustman. As a result, Doolittle has been left three thousand pounds a year (a huge sum in those days) provided that he gives lectures on request for the Wannafeller Moral Reform World League.

Higgins and Pickering are amused, the latter remarking that Doolittle will not be invited to speak more than once! But Doolittle is not amused at all: he considers that his whole way of life has been destroyed. He explains at length. As one of the undeserving poor, he could scrounge money from people whenever he wanted to, free from the attentions of solicitors, doctors, servants and relations. Now that he has become a gentleman, all these people flock around badgering him with their services, for which they expect money. He even suspects that Higgins may have set the whole thing up just to earn fees for teaching him to speak 'middle class language'. He is no longer free. His happiness has gone.

Mrs Higgins points out that he could simply refuse the bequest and remain as he was. But Doolittle explains that he is frightened of an old age spent in a workhouse. If he had been one of the deserving poor, he might have had a few savings put by for his old age, but the careful deserving poor are no happier than millionaires. He is caught between the fear of the workhouse and the misery of being middle class and he hasn't the nerve for the workhouse. His life is broken – and it is all Higgins's fault!

Doolittle's spirited defence of the way of life of the undeserving poor in Act Two has been capped by his comically tragic reappearance in Act Five. Of course we laugh at his predicament and his explanation of it, but the fear of ending one's days in the workhouse was a nightmare to very many poor people and reminds us of the harsh social conditions of the time. Doolittle also provides another example of what happens to a person suddenly jerked out of his social class. The same thing has happened to Eliza and she, in her own way, is equally disorientated. But by the end of this act we are going to see a development in her mind and personality which will enable her to cope with the situation, whereas her father will remain an unhappy rich man, living in comfort but regretting the old life that 'had some ginger in it'.

When Mrs Higgins says that Doolittle is now in a position to provide for his daughter, Higgins reacts vigorously. Since he has paid for her she no longer belongs to Doolittle. Mrs Higgins reveals that Eliza is upstairs, whereupon Higgins marches to the door intent on bringing her down. Mrs Higgins now takes charge. Rising from her seat, she calls her son back to sit down and listen to her. She spells out very clearly the two men's lack of concern for Eliza's feelings after her success at the ambassador's party and their failure to thank or praise her. Pickering is repentant but Higgins makes no apology and is furious when his mother says that Eliza refuses to return to Wimpole Street but is willing to meet him 'on friendly terms and let bygones be bygones' (p. 119). Mrs Higgins asks Doolittle to wait outside on the balcony until Eliza has made things up with the men.

A few moments later, Eliza enters the room. This is very much her scene and is a moment for getting her own back on Higgins. He is at a disadvantage in being angry and boorish while Eliza is completely in control of herself, 'giving a staggeringly convincing exhibition of ease of manner' (p. 120). She talks almost entirely to Colonel Pickering, thanking him for showing her by his example the meaning of good manners, and how ladies and gentlemen should behave. Completely ignored, Higgins seethes with anger. When the Colonel tries to give Higgins the credit for teaching her correct speech, she dismisses this by saying it is merely his profession, on a par with being a dancing master. She drives home her attack on Higgins by thanking Pickering for the many small courtesies from which she has learnt so much and which have given her self-respect. She shrewdly observes that the difference between a lady and a flower girl is not how she behaves but how she is treated (p. 122). Her final thrust is to ask Pickering (who has always addressed her as Miss Doolittle) to call her Eliza, whereas she wants Higgins to call her Miss Doolittle.

This brings Higgins back into the centre of the scene and he explodes angrily. Calmly, Eliza refuses to indulge in a slanging match with him, saying that she cannot do it any more. Like a child in a foreign country who picks up a new language quickly, this is all that Eliza can speak. She has quite forgotten the language of Tottenham Court Road; leaving Wimpole Street has completed the process. Higgins's declaration that without him beside her she will be back in the gutter in three weeks is met by Eliza's confident assertion that she could not utter one of her old cries if she tried.

Shaw has beautifully contrived this moment of pride before a fall. Everything has so far gone entirely Eliza's way. Higgins's 'live doll' has put him in his place with devastating effect, his skill as a teacher reduced to less importance in her eyes than Pickering's good manners. Suddenly the effect is shattered: Doolittle enters in his finery and startles Eliza into her old cry of 'A-a-a-a-a-ah-ow-ooh!' Higgins is wild with delight, his point apparently proved. The old Eliza lies only just below her new veneer.

Eliza is upset that her father is going to marry her so-called step-mother, 'that low common woman'. It appears that the wife-to-be is as intimidated as Doolittle and has decided to conform to the dictates of middle-class morality. Doolittle asks his daughter to attend the wedding and she leaves the room to get ready.

As they wait, Doolittle asks Pickering to come with him to the wedding. Pickering of course agrees and the conversation gives Doolittle the opportunity for one more comic stab at middle-class morality. He reveals that this is his first marriage, since he never actually married Eliza's mother. 'That aint the natural way, Colonel: it's only the middle class way' (p. 124). Mrs Higgins pleases him by asking if she may attend his wedding and, as Eliza returns, she goes off to prepare to go to the church. Before he leaves the stage, Doolittle sums up Eliza's situation as he sees it. Because she was in the care of two gentlemen rather than one, she was never able to 'nail' either of them (presumably into marriage). Doolittle considers these to be extremely cunning tactics on the men's part and, as one who has suffered from the wiles of women all his life, he does not grudge the men their success. Before he leaves for Doolittle's wedding, Pickering begs Eliza to forgive Higgins and come back with them to Wimpole Street.

The stage is thus cleared of the other characters, leaving Eliza and Higgins for their final confrontation. So far Eliza has learned to speak and behave enough like a duchess to convince the guests at an ambassador's party. As we have just seen, she has also become sufficiently confident to conduct a battle of wits against Higgins in his mother's drawing room and win it hands down – or until the moment of Doolittle's appearance. But the basic problems remain unsolved: first, is she, as Higgins believes, unable to exist in her new social class without his support?; second, if she leaves him, how will she survive financially?; third, what is to be the nature of her relationship with Higgins himself in the future? Pygmalion has created his masterpiece (see p. 67), but is his Galatea to be permanently dependent on her creator or can she truly become a woman, totally independent of him? This is the essence of the discussion that follows (pp. 126–33) and its development in detail is worth close study.

At first, Eliza does not want to be alone with Higgins but he reaches the door before her and forces her into conversation with him. Eliza believes he will try to cajole her into returning to Wimpole Street to fetch and carry for him. Higgins points out that he has never asked her to come back. If she comes, it will make no difference to his behaviour or manners. What he considers important is having the same manners towards everybody, high or low in the social scale. He may treat her rudely, but has she ever heard him treat anyone else differently?

Eliza now makes clear one aspect of her dissatisfaction with him when she says, 'I wont be passed over' (p. 126). Higgins is not impressed and Eliza is driven to declare, 'I can get on without you'. At present this is an idle boast, but Higgins takes the wind out of her sails by replying that he knows she can and he has told her so before. Eliza is hurt by this and claims he made that remark when he wanted to get rid of her, which he denies.

A change of mood comes about when Higgins asks whether she ever considered if he could do without her. He admits that he will miss her, that he has learned from her 'idiotic notions' and he has grown accustomed to her voice and appearance – and rather likes them. No photographs or recordings could replace her soul: 'they are not you' (p. 127).

Eliza considers that Higgins is using his skill with words merely to tempt her back for his own sake, when he does not really care for her at all. He replies that he cares for life and she is a part of it that has come his way. Understandably, this does not satisfy Eliza who declares she will not care for anyone who does not care for her. Higgins regards this notion as mere commercialism, the buying and selling of affection, and he rejects it. He has no use for a woman who tries to win his favour by behaving like a slave. If Eliza wants to resume living in his house, it must be for good fellowship and for no other reason. This is as far as he will go, but for Eliza this is not enough; she wants a warmer response. Why did he train her if he did not care for her? 'Why, because it was my job,' he replies. He refuses to acknowledge any warmer emotion and insists that he will continue with his work and his way of life. She can come back or go to the devil, just as she pleases.

Eliza is still deeply troubled. Higgins's attitude that she would come back simply for the fun of it and that they could walk out on each other at any time brings her up sharply against her old dilemma. She cannot go back to selling flowers. She has lost her independence: 'I'm a slave now, for all my fine clothes' (p. 129).

Higgins disagrees. He could adopt her as his daughter; Pickering might even marry her. This infuriates Eliza: she is not looking for some arranged marriage. She would have no problem finding suitors:

Freddy Eynsford Hill, for instance, writes to her every day. Higgins is most displeased to hear that Eliza has not discouraged Freddy, for whom he has only contempt.

The possibility of Eliza even considering the attentions of Freddy has introduced a new element into the scene. It leads the two characters into a vigorous statement of their own attitudes and brings to a crisis the clash between Higgins's cold intellectual approach to life and Eliza's desire for a warm human relationship. It also raises directly the possibility of a love affair between them when Higgins says, 'In short, you want me to be as infatuated about you as Freddy, is that it?' (p. 130). Eliza denies this but has difficulty in expressing her feelings. She admits to being 'only a common ignorant girl' but she is not dirt under his feet. She would like a little kindness. She went through the training sessions because they were pleasant together and she 'came to care for him'.

We should note here how Eliza makes errors of speech as she becomes something again of the 'squashed cabbage leaf' of the opening scenes, all too aware of her inadequacy. It makes all the more effective her sudden triumph a minute or two later. This is stimulated by Higgins's speech (p. 130) contemptuously dismissing her to the so-called 'real' life of the gutter, if that is what she wants. He tells her that if she cannot stand the coldness of his intellectual way of life, she had better marry 'some sentimental hog or other with lots of money and a thick pair of lips to kiss you with and a thick pair of boots to kick you with'.

The heartlessness and brutal tone of this speech rouse Eliza to desperation. She shows how wicked and cruel he is to suggest she could ever return to the gutter after her life with him and Pickering, the only friends she has in the world. But he has not got her under his feet. As soon as she can support him, she will marry Freddy! This sudden decision horrifies and dismays Higgins who claims he has made her into a consort for a king, not for a young man who cannot even earn his own living. For Eliza, however, Freddy offers the one thing that Higgins's way of life denies: 'Freddy loves me'.

Yet she will have to earn a living for them both and suddenly Eliza sees how it can be done! She does after all have an ability that will give her the independence she craves: she will become a teacher and use all the knowledge she has gained from Higgins. She will become an assistant to a despised rival teacher of phonetics. Higgins is so angry that he seizes hold of her, but only for a moment, being even more angry at his loss of temper, while Eliza triumphs over him. She will teach anybody to be a duchess in six months for a thousand guineas. She is as good as he is.

Higgins's anger is replaced by wonder and excitement as he realizes the real success of his experiment. Eliza is not simply a puppet who can speak and behave well under his direction: she has become a free woman, totally independent of him and able to make her own way in upper-middle-class society. He invites her to join Pickering and himself in Wimpole Street on equal terms as 'three old bachelors'.

Mrs Higgins returns, ready for Doolittle's wedding and Eliza formally bids Higgins farewell saying, 'Then I shall not see you again, Professor'. Higgins, in his usual manner, chooses to ignore this completely and cheerfully issues Eliza with a number of orders for shopping. Eliza corrects him on several details and, in her efficient way, has already dealt with most of the matters. 'What you are to do without me I cannot imagine,' she says as she departs. Mrs Higgins's hint of the possibility of marriage between Eliza and Pickering is drowned in Higgins's uproarious laughter as he tells her, 'Pickering! Nonsense: she's going to marry Freddy'.

In the Greek legend, Galatea married her Pygmalion. Shaw resists this romantic ending for Eliza and Higgins (even though so many audiences would like to see the conventional happy ending implied in the film version). One can see Shaw's point. If Eliza married Higgins, there would be no clear sign that she really had become entirely independent of him. This is the point of the play: without intending to do so or realizing it would happen, Higgins has created someone far more impressive than a duchess – a free and independent woman.

## Scenes from the Film

Shaw was always interested in the possibility of transferring his plays to the screen but he was chary of letting film directors and script writers loose on his work without his own close control. Two film

versions of *Pygmalion* – one German (1935), the other Dutch (1937) –
had greatly disappointed him because of the liberties that had been
taken with his play, especially the insistence on linking Higgins and
Eliza romantically. He resisted offers from several leading producers
for the rights to make an English version, but at last gave the contract
to Gabriel Pascal, a Hungarian film producer who had won Shaw's
friendship and confidence.

The film had its première in London in 1938 and was a great
success. Shaw had written the script himself, introducing scenes not
in his original play, the longest and most important being the embassy
ball at which Eliza wins Higgins's bet. He made several alterations to
his original, designed to strengthen Freddy's position as a suitor and
to eliminate any suggestion that Higgins would eventually marry
Eliza, even writing two alternative final scenes to make this absolutely
clear.

Ironically, even Gabriel Pascal could not resist the pressure for a
romantic ending. The film-makers contrived their own ending without writing any new dialogue. At the very end of the film, Higgins
comes home alone and accidentally turns on a recording of Eliza's
voice. When he switches it off, he hears Eliza's real voice; she has
entered the room and is standing behind him. Without turning
around, he asks her for his slippers. Her expression suggests the
happy romantic ending that the public was believed to want. Shaw
only saw the film two days before its public première and could do
nothing about it. He undoubtedly disapproved of the ending but, as
the rest of the film was so faithful to his script, he accepted it with a
good grace. Leslie Howard played the part of Higgins. As a film star
associated with romantic parts, Howard was not Shaw's choice, and
he did not like his performance. But Shaw insisted on a young, virtually
unknown actress named Wendy Hiller for Eliza. She scored an enormous success in the part and went on to a long and distinguished
career in the English theatre. If you have a chance to see the film,
take the opportunity. It is of the greatest interest to students of the
play.

In view of the success of the film, Shaw prepared an edition of the
play (first published by Penguin in 1941) which included some
material from his film script. He also wrote prose passages to link the
film sequences to the original play. These appear in the following

pages of the current Penguin edition, pp. 30–32, 46–9, 63–5, 85–95, 105–10. We will discuss them in turn.

*pp. 30–32*: this short section covers Eliza's return home by taxi after she leaves St Paul's, Covent Garden. The most important thing to note is the poverty of Eliza's surroundings. Apart from a bird-cage and two pin-ups, her room and its furnishings are described as 'the irreducible minimum of poverty's needs'. A few lines later we are told of Eliza's 'gnawing sense of the need for economy'. In order to make their leading lady attractive, the film-makers (and often theatrical directors, too) fail to make Eliza as dirty and poverty-stricken as Shaw intended. Yet the transformation of Eliza is all the more effective if at the start she really is seen to be a 'draggletailed gutter-snipe'.

*pp. 46–9*: half way through Act Two, Eliza is taken away by Mrs Pearce to be bathed. The film sequence shows Eliza's horror at being forced to take off all her clothes and immerse herself in water. There is, of course, comedy in Eliza's amazement at her new bedroom and the bathroom and at her reluctance to undress, but there is also implied comment on the social conditions of the poor, who rarely washed and were usually too cold to undress at night. Note, too, Mrs Pearce's blunt description of Eliza as 'a frowzy slut'.

*pp. 63–5*: here we are given a glimpse of Higgins's teaching methods as he trains Eliza to speak 'like a duchess'. His style ranges characteristically from severe bullying to rewarding his pupil with a chocolate. Eliza is swift to copy his speech – her quick ear is a factor in her success. All the same, this does not seem a very convincing speech lesson. Very little is achieved and the lesson is mostly occupied with Higgins showing off. We must presume his other speech lessons were more effective.

*pp. 85–95*: this section is the most considerable of the additions for the film script and it introduces a new character of some interest in the person of Nepommuck, formerly a pupil of Higgins and now a rival teacher of speech. (It is with Nepommuck that Eliza proposes to work as a teacher after the end of the play (p. 131).) Higgins and Pickering are waiting in the hall of the embassy for Eliza to come from the ladies' cloakroom when he is approached and then embraced by a whiskery young man whom he at first fails to recognize. The young man reminds him that he is his most famous pupil, 'little

Nepommuck, the marvellous boy'. He can speak thirty-two languages and now earns his living training social upstarts how to disguise their origins and speak good English. Like Higgins, he is expert at placing people by their accents. He therefore poses a real threat to Eliza.

Eliza joins Higgins and Pickering and they mount the stairs to be presented to the ambassador and his wife. The hostess assumes Eliza is Pickering's adopted daughter and declares she will create a sensation. When her guests move on, she tells Nepommuck to find out all he can about her.

As she moves like a sleep-walker through the crowded salons, Eliza does indeed create a sensation; people stand on chairs to gaze at her. At last the ambassador's wife asks Professor Higgins who the girl really is. Before he can reply, Nepommuck arrives, saying he knows all about Eliza and declaring her to be a fraud. For a moment it seems that Higgins has lost his bet, but Nepommuck has made a mistake. He declares that Eliza speaks English so perfectly that she must be a well-taught foreigner: he believes her to be a Hungarian princess. When asked for his opinion, Higgins says she is 'an ordinary London girl out of the gutter and taught to speak by an expert'. Nobody pays any attention to Higgins's opinion. Higgins is first joined by Pickering and then by Eliza, who apologizes to Higgins for losing his bet. But Pickering assures her she has won handsomely. All three are glad to leave the party.

It would be unthinkable for a film-maker to omit the scene of Eliza's triumph, with the opportunity it gives for spectacle and the excitement of seeing how Eliza will fare in high society. The 1938 film embellished the scene still further by adding to the company at the embassy ball an elderly lady of royal birth and her very handsome son. The climax came when this Prince Charming asked Eliza to dance with him, which she did to the admiration of all present. But this is quite irrelevant to the play and places too much emphasis on to the winning of the bet. The real point of the play is what will happen to Eliza once her speech and manners have been changed from a flower girl's to a lady's.

Nepommuck is an interesting figure and he is discussed in the section on characters on p. 66.

*pp. 105–10*: this scene bridges the gap between Eliza's leaving the room in Wimpole Street late at night and her arrival at Mrs Higgins's house. Eliza changes her evening dress for outdoor clothing and leaves Higgins's house, slamming the door behind her. Outside she finds the love-sick Freddy who apparently spends most of his nights gazing at her window. They embrace passionately until they are interrupted by an elderly police constable. Freddy announces that they have just become engaged and they run away to Cavendish Square, where Eliza confesses to Freddy that her original intention had been to throw herself into the river. They embrace again and declare their love for each other, only to be halted again, this time by a younger constable. Once more they run away, embrace again and then take refuge in a passing taxi. They propose to drive around all night until Eliza can call on Mrs Higgins in the morning and ask her what she ought to do.

Although as unnecessary to the stage play as all the other film additions, this scene does build up the character of Freddy as a future husband for Eliza. Indeed, he announces their engagement during this scene. Their frequent embraces show clearly their desire for each other – thus making a nonsense of ending the film with the suggestion of a romance between Eliza and Higgins.

# Characters

---

## PROFESSOR HIGGINS

Shaw describes Higgins in the stage direction on p. 34. He is a 'robust, vital, appetizing sort of man of forty or thereabouts . . . He is of the energetic scientific type, heartily, even violently interested in everything that can be studied as a scientific subject and careless about himself and other people, including their feelings . . .'

All this is borne out in the play. Higgins's life is devoted to the science of speech. He has a laboratory in his own house, he goes out into the streets with his notebook to record people's accents and Mrs Pearce, his housekeeper, has grown accustomed to 'such queer people' coming to see him in order to talk into his recording machines. For him this study is all-absorbing and he has no patience with anything that stands in its way.

He certainly has no time for social conventions. His mother is dismayed when he comes to her at-home because, as she says, 'You offend all my friends: they stop coming whenever they meet you'. Polite society irritates him with its veneer of good manners, which, in his opinion, hides emptiness and ignorance. He gives vent to his feelings in Act Three as the company awaits the arrival of Eliza: 'You see, we're all savages more or less. We're supposed to be civilized and cultured – to know all about poetry and philosophy and art and science, and so on; but how many of us know even the meaning of these names?' (p. 73).

It is ironic that, with such views, he earns his living by seeming to pander to this falseness. He tells Pickering that in an age of upstarts he can teach the men who began in Kentish Town with £80 and end up in Park Lane with a hundred thousand how to change the accents which reveal their humble origins. Yet he could, if he wished, justify his work in what he says to his mother in Act Three (p. 82) where, speaking of Eliza, he claims that one can change a person 'into a quite different human being by creating a new speech for her. It's filling up the deepest gulf that separates class from class and soul from soul.' (Whether the upstarts from Kentish Town would see it that way is a matter not pursued in the play.)

Higgins's absorbing interest in his scientific investigations makes him, as Shaw says, 'careless about himself and other people, including their feelings'. In Act Two (pp. 50–52) Mrs Pearce lists his domestic failings, such as eating everything off one plate and wiping his fingers on his dressing gown, while his swearing is remarked on at various times by Mrs Pearce, Mrs Higgins and Pickering. More serious is his disregard of people's feelings. There is evidence of this in the ungracious way he speaks to the Eynsford Hills during the at-home, but much more important is the way he behaves to Eliza.

His disregard for her feelings is a central feature of the play and – although Higgins neither realizes it nor intends it – part of the process by which she learns to stand on her own feet. Higgins first meets Eliza in the portico of St Paul's church and he is really only interested in her accent. As her grumbling distracts Higgins from his conversation with Pickering, he rebukes her for 'crooning like a bilious pigeon', talks of her as 'this creature with her kerbstone English' and addresses her as 'you squashed cabbage leaf, you disgrace to the noble architecture of these columns, you incarnate insult to the English language . . .' A day later at Wimpole Street he describes her to her face as 'so deliciously low, so horribly dirty', calls her a baggage, talks of her as 'this draggletailed guttersnipe', tells Mrs Pearce to accommodate her in the dustbin if necessary and threatens her with a broomstick! It is an astonishing catalogue of insults. Nowhere at all does he show any regard for Eliza's feelings. He discusses her with Pickering and takes a bet on her as though she were some object from another world. He quite callously remarks that she will need no money: 'She'll only drink if you give her money' (p. 43). When Pickering remonstrates – 'Does it occur to you, Higgins, that the girl has some feelings?' – Higgins replies, 'Oh no. I don't think so. Not any feelings that we need bother about . . .' Little wonder that Eliza comments shortly afterwards, 'Oh, youve no feeling heart in you: you dont care for nothing but yourself'.

His insensitivity to Eliza's feelings leads to the crisis in Act Four after the bet has been won. When the crisis is over, Higgins leaves the room, slamming the door savagely and Eliza goes upstairs in a tearing rage. We have to wait until the final pages of Act Five for a calmer appraisal of their attitudes. Even here Higgins will yield nothing: 'I cant change my nature; and I dont intend to change my manners' (p. 126). A little later he says, 'The great secret, Eliza, is not having bad manners or good manners or any other particular sort of manners, but having the same manner for all human souls'. This attitude, however fine it sounds, does not satisfy Eliza and it may not satisfy us. What Higgins seems to be demanding is something almost superhuman – a life of good fellowship on equal terms ('You and I and Pickering will be three old bachelors') – with complete individual independence and with no ties or concessions to human feelings. He explains his position in the speech (p. 130) contrasting the life of Science, Literature and Art with the life of the gutter: 'It's real: it's warm: it's violent'. The speech is powerful but unfair and it provokes Eliza to her most defiant statement: 'I'll marry Freddy, I will . . .' Freddy, for all his weakness, offers her the simple love and affection she craves.

Higgins's chosen way of life elevates the intellect and scientific interests above any human feeling. For him such a life is stimulating and exciting; it is 'fun' as far as he is concerned. He possesses enormous vitality – like a motor bus 'all bounce and go, and no consideration for anyone', as Eliza says (p. 127) – and this sweeps him along. But it will not satisfy Eliza, nor most other people. Higgins is a special person.

How has Higgins become such a person? In his stage direction (p. 34) Shaw speaks of him as 'rather like a very impetuous baby, "taking notice" eagerly and loudly, and requiring almost as much watching to keep him out of unintended mischief'. The word 'babylike' recurs in the stage direction at the top of page 37 and Mrs Higgins refers to Pickering and her son as 'a couple of babies' (p. 81). The pampered child in Higgins is a part of his character and must be related to his strong attachment to his mother, his impatience with young women and his refusal to marry unless he can find his ideal – someone as like his mother as possible. There are two mother-figures in the play. One is Mrs Higgins herself, wise, calm and understanding. She does not interfere in her son's life, but she is his ideal and the one to whom he turns in moments of crisis. The other mother-figure is Mrs Pearce, who fulfils the day-to-day role of keeping him in order, running his house, rebuking him for his bad manners and trying (usually in vain) to make him act sensibly in ordinary affairs. Mrs Higgins is thus able to remain a benevolent figure, removed from the anxieties of daily caring for this wayward son.

Money has also been an important reason for the way that Higgins has managed to maintain his self-centred existence so happily. He is financially and socially secure. He need not feel 'intimidated', like Doolittle: he has plenty of money and a sure position in middle-class society. He may criticize that society's way of life, its conventions, manners and morality, and set himself apart from it; but he lives comfortably in his large house with servants, free to indulge his interest in scientific research, quite unconcerned about manners because he does not need to impress or influence anyone else. He is rich enough not to care. Eliza's situation is precisely the opposite. She has no position in middle-class society and no money at all. Higgins's resolute refusal to take any notice of this ultimately drives Eliza to desperation. Only when she sees how she can earn money as a teacher can she break free of Higgins. Financial security is the key to a freer life, unless, like Doolittle, you opt for the freedom of being an undeserving scrounger, with the shadow of the workhouse ahead.

Higgins's insensitivity and bad manners could make him into a very unattractive person yet this is not the case. As Shaw says in his stage direction (p. 34), '. . . he is so entirely frank and void of malice that he remains likeable even in his least reasonable moments'. There is no doubt about his frankness: he says bluntly what he feels, regardless of others. But his frank remarks are not uttered with any intention to wound (however hurtful they may seem to the recipient). To those who know him, he can be infuriatingly unreasonable but never spiteful or wicked. His bluntness arises from a total preoccupation with his own interests and an unwillingness to suffer fools gladly. He is also a person of rapidly changing moods, so that an outburst can be followed by gentle persuasive talk that can begin to heal the wounds. Examples of this are to be found on pages 42 and 127. Higgins certainly has charm and this quality has appealed to audiences – and to leading actors who have played him on stage and screen – over the years.

What are Higgins's feelings for Eliza? Shaw never tired of emphasizing that there was to be no romance between them and the play contains very few remarks that can be construed as anything beyond a desire for 'good fellowship'. Yet when in Act Five Eliza calls Higgins a devil who could twist the heart of a girl, it is her reaction to the unexpected remark, 'I shall miss you, Eliza. I have learnt something from your idiotic notions: I confess that humbly and gratefully. And I have grown accustomed to your voice and appearance. I like them rather' (p. 127). Eliza scornfully tells him he has recordings and photographs of her, to which he replies, '. . . I can't turn your soul on. Leave me those feelings; and you can take away the voice and the face. They are not you'. Eliza sees this as an attempt to get round her but, having gone this far in admitting a personal feeling for her, Higgins withdraws into the explanation that he cares for life, for humanity and that she is a part of it which has come his way and been built into his house. He tells her to '. . . come back for the sake of good fellowship; for youll get nothing else' (p. 128). This is a long way from the natural human feelings that Eliza is seeking and which she finds in Freddy; yet the scene does contain a hint that Eliza has come to mean something to Higgins. But he refuses to take it further than that.

Finally we must ask how successful Higgins is as Pygmalion. Can he really take the credit for creating a real woman out of a 'squashed cabbage leaf'? No doubt Eliza would have remained in the gutter all her life if he had not taken her into his home and changed her speech, clothed her fashionably and shown her how the middle and upper classes behaved (although Pickering is given much credit for this by Eliza). Yet it is worth considering at the point at which the bet has been won, what kind of person Higgins has created. In the note from the film sequence (p. 93), Shaw speaks of Eliza at the reception as walking 'like a somnambulist in a desert'. From her remarks in Acts Four and Five she obviously does not consider herself a part of the society in which she has won the bet, but merely an 'artificial duchess' for a night, a phrase used by Higgins (p. 99). Higgins's achievement has been to create something quite unnatural and out of place. His mother spoke of the two men as babies playing with their live doll. The doll-like quality of Eliza is most evident in her first public appearance at Mrs Higgins's at-home. She moves like an automaton through the introductions and her reply to Mrs Higgins's remark about the rain reminds us of a tape-recorded weather report. Only when she begins to relax does she – with comic effect – allow the warm reality of her life in the slums to break through the artifice of her speech. Higgins has created a doll, a sleep-walker, an 'artificial duchess' – no more. The real personality of Eliza from Drury Lane has been suppressed to produce the mere outward appearance of a lady. No wonder Higgins himself found it such a bore! His form of education, far from being life-enhancing, actually takes away the real vitality that Eliza had in abundance.

Only when driven to desperation about her future and Higgins's lack of concern over her does Eliza find the key to independence through the idea of marrying Freddy and supporting them both by teaching. Then, fully herself at last , she can celebrate her triumph over Higgins in her natural language, 'Thats done you, Enry Iggins, it az'. When Higgins realizes what has happened, he 'wonders at her' (as the stage direction on p. 132 indicates), as well he might. Characteristically, he claims the credit: 'By George, Eliza, I said I'd make a woman of you; and I have'. But it is not true. Circumstances (in which admittedly he played a part) and Eliza's own character have achieved the transformation. In the classical legend, Pygmalion had to beg the goddess to bring his creation to life: for Higgins, his Galatea has achieved the miracle herself.

## COLONEL PICKERING

Colonel Pickering is a secondary character but he is socially as well as dramatically necessary, because Higgins on his own could hardly pick up a girl from the streets and instal her in his house without being suspected of improper motives. With the very correct Colonel Pickering, together with Mrs Pearce, living in the house as well, this difficulty is removed.

Pickering is more than simply a guarantor of respectability. A student of spoken language himself ('the author of Spoken Sanscrit'), he has a very real interest in Higgins's work and he challenges Higgins to fulfil his boast that he can transform Eliza into a duchess. Moreover, he undertakes to pay the bills.

In a play so full of parallels and contrasts (see p. 71), Pickering serves as a foil to Higgins: he is courteous and considerate where Higgins is mannerless and insensitive. Eliza reckons that her education as a lady began when Pickering first called her 'Miss Doolittle' (p. 45). In Act Five she remarks, 'That was the beginning of self-respect for me'. In the same scene she gives him considerable credit, not just for his generosity in paying for her clothes but for teaching her good manners through his personal example: 'I know I can be a lady to you, because you always treat me like a lady, and always will' (p. 122).

Pickering is very typical of the upper middle class. His background and education was 'Cheltenham, Harrow, Cambridge and India', he has now retired from the army and returned home to England, apparently with the express intention of seeking out the celebrated Professor Higgins. Higgins, in turn, has admired Pickering's work sufficiently to plan a visit to India to meet him! (p. 28). Despite this, Pickering plays no part in the technical speech education of Eliza: his role is to be a companion for Higgins with whom he can discuss Eliza, and a partner who can accompany Higgins when he takes Eliza out – for example, to the at-home or the ambassador's party.

Courteous and considerate though Pickering is, he acts and speaks with the conscious superiority of the upper classes. The bystanders in Act One are aware of his social position and believe that the note taker is unlikely to be caught 'taking liberties with a gentleman' (p. 24). In fact the two gentlemen get on very well together and Pickering becomes Higgins's guest, but this does not prevent him from asking for firm assurances about Eliza's position in the house and supporting Mrs Pearce in her pleas for Higgins to make sensible arrangements for the girl. There are only two lapses from his natural courtesy, as when he joins Higgins in making up a silly rhyme about Eliza's name (p. 39). The other is his failure (dramatically necessary) to congratulate and thank Eliza on her success at the beginning of Act Four.

Pickering's views on morality are conventional. He is clearly troubled that Doolittle is not married to his 'missus'. He says, 'I rather draw the line at encouraging that sort of immorality' (p. 59). It is fitting that Doolittle chooses him to be a witness at his wedding when this matter is put right.

Where Eliza's situation is concerned, Pickering is at first more prepared than Higgins to consider practicalities. But by the time Eliza visits Mrs Higgins he seems to have become infected with Higgins's own reluctance to consider the girl's future. When Mrs Higgins confronts them with the problem of Eliza, he is rather bored by it and assures her vaguely that 'There are plenty of openings. We'll do whats right' (p. 84). He also supports Higgins in reporting Eliza's departure to the police 'as if she were a thief or a lost umbrella, or something' (pp. 112–13).

He is a more sympathetic person than Higgins and one feels that genuine affection develops between Eliza and himself. Mrs Higgins notes this at the very end of the play when she says to her son, 'I should be uneasy about you and her if she were less fond of Colonel Pickering'. His final words to Eliza are, 'Do stay with us, Eliza', and we feel sure he means it.

## MRS HIGGINS

Mrs Higgins, the mother of Professor Higgins, is a lady with a comfortable and assured position in society. She has taste – as we see from the decoration and furnishings of her drawing room (p. 66) – and, unlike the Eynsford Hills, plenty of money to support her position. In character she is gracious, considerate and unfailingly polite; but she is also firm and well in control of the situation, as those who visit her at home discover.

One of her functions in the play is to preside over two important scenes – Eliza's visit to her at-home in Act Three (pp. 73–8) and the first part of Act Five when Higgins finds that Eliza has sought refuge in his mother's house. In the first of these scenes, she does all she can to keep the social event as normal as possible despite the unexpected arrival of Eliza, treating her with great courtesy and refusing to react either to her 'Not bloody likely' or to Clara's 'Such bloody nonsense'! She clearly contemplates asking Eliza to visit her again for she invites Freddy to come another afternoon to see her.

In Act Five she again insists on the social niceties and in so doing calms a stormy situation. For example, when Doolittle bursts into the room in his finery and launches bitterly into Higgins, Mrs Higgins quietly says, 'Good morning, Mr Doolittle. Wont you sit down?', thus restoring order to the discussion. A little later Higgins is about to rush upstairs to fetch Eliza by force: Mrs Higgins tells him very firmly to sit down and listen to what she has to say. In such ways she ensures that all the characters behave with social correctness, however strong their personal feelings.

Her relationship with her son is most important. He loves and admires her greatly: 'My idea of a lovable woman is somebody as like you as possible'. In matters of behaviour she can still treat him as a small boy – 'Stop fidgeting and take your hands out of your pockets. Thats a good boy' (p. 68) – but she is shrewd and clear-sighted about practical affairs, in complete contrast to her son. After the 'at-home', she makes the obvious judgement about Eliza: 'You silly boy, of course she's not presentable' (p. 80). She goes on to inquire about the position of Eliza in Higgins's household and sums up the naïve enthusiasm of her son and Colonel Pickering with 'You certainly are a pretty pair of babies, playing with your live doll'. A little later, she puts her finger on the central question – one constantly ignored by Higgins – of what is to be done with Eliza after the experiment is over (p. 84). When she questions the value of the so-called advantages Higgins has given Eliza, he and Pickering brush them aside.

In Act Five Mrs Higgins stage-manages the scene, keeping Eliza in her room until she is ready for her. The arrival of Doolittle, unexpectedly transformed by his dress into a rich man, seems to Mrs Higgins to solve the problem of Eliza's future now that he can provide for her. At this point she reveals that Eliza is upstairs in her house; but before she sends the maid for her she sets out very clearly the ways in which the two men have failed either to understand Eliza's feelings or to treat her with kindness and consideration. Typically, she will not send for Eliza until Higgins promises to behave himself in front of the girl. In the encounter that follows, she adds little beyond one or two reminders to her son about his behaviour, but all the characters are aware of her presence. With her usual sensitivity, she asks Doolittle if she may attend his wedding, thereby soothing a little the feelings of the unhappy bridegroom.

Mrs Higgins reappears at the very end of the play, ready to leave for the wedding (p. 132). Her remark about her concern for Higgins if Eliza were less fond of Colonel Pickering (p. 133) shows that, for all her practical understanding, she still sees marriage as a woman's natural goal. She has no idea of what has been really happening to the soul of Eliza nor of her growth towards true independence as a human being.

## ELIZA

In the Pygmalion legend (see p. 67), Galatea begins her existence as a block of stone. Higgins regards Eliza as little better – in his case a squashed cabbage leaf with no feelings worth bothering about. But he is wrong. Eliza's spirited personality is clear from the moment of her arrival in the portico of St Paul's church. Freddy knocks her basket of flowers from her hand and she protests vigorously, giving his mother a piece of her mind, too (p. 16). The suggestion that the note taker might be a police informer makes her protest loudly to try and establish her rights: 'You just shew me what youve wrote about me' (p. 22). She is certainly not a young woman to be 'put upon' and, although she falls to grumbling while the gentlemen talk, she is capable of flinging her whole basket of flowers at the feet of Higgins in a grand gesture of desperation. Most significant of all in this first act is her sudden decision to hire a taxi. As soon as she has money, she spends it on one of the pleasures in life, until then quite beyond her means.

In a reversal of the myth, this Galatea chooses her Pygmalion. Eliza seeks out Professor Higgins and applies for lessons on her own initiative. His casual boast to Pickering that he could pass her off as a duchess has not fallen on deaf ears. The girl who instantly spends her money on the luxury of a taxi has registered the possibility – fantastic though it might seem – that this strange man can transform her life. She does not hesitate. She will spend what would be an enormous portion of her usual income on the necessary lessons.

What is Eliza's motive? Never for a moment do we feel that Eliza is simply after money to pay for the luxuries of taxis, chocolates and jewels. The furthest extent of her ambition when she goes to see Higgins is to be 'a lady in a flower shop'. But the important thing is that she is aware there is more to life than selling flowers in Tottenham Court Road. Given an opportunity to better herself, she takes it immediately.

Her background is truly depressing, a social comment on the life of the poor. Eliza has been 'educated' with the lick of her father's strap, turned out by her parents to fend for herself and now is living alone in a squalid room; her daily income is not enough to keep herself clean and reasonably clothed. Though in Higgins's view, she is 'deliciously low – so horribly dirty', she has the courage to try and tidy herself up, putting on her hat with the three ostrich feathers and then daring to call on Higgins at his home in fashionable Wimpole Street. This action alone shows that Eliza has unusual qualities. What other flower girl would have been brave enough to enter this strange world of ladies and gentlemen and bargain with a professor over the price of lessons?

Things are not made easier for her by Higgins's boorish manners. A few moments of conversation establish him in her mind as 'barmy' and soon she is heading for the door, expressing early in their acquaintance a central theme of the play: 'Oh, youve no feeling heart in you: you dont care for nothing but yourself' (p. 44). Thoroughly confused by all that is being said, she allows herself to be taken away for a bath, lamenting, 'If I'd known what I was letting myself in for, I wouldnt have come here'. But she has come and her life is about to be changed.

The training of Eliza involves self-discipline on her part and a great deal of unaccustomed brain work. Mrs Higgins spells this out in Act Five (p. 118): 'She worked very hard for you, Henry. I dont think you quite realize what anything in the nature of brain work means to a girl of her class'. But Eliza has persevered and she is quick on the uptake. Higgins speaks of her quickness of ear (p. 82) but adds, characteristically, 'just like a parrot'. But Pickering tells Mrs Higgins that 'that girl is a genius' and instances her remarkable ability to play the piano by ear.

It is ironic, therefore, that such natural talent is devoted to producing something as unreal as the dressed-up doll trying to converse at Mrs Higgins's at-home, and the 'artificial duchess' at the ambassador's reception. At the beginning of Act Four, Eliza knows very well that she is not a flower girl, but the fuller life of which she dreams continues to elude her. Her future is more empty and meaningless than it was in Drury Lane. She has allowed herself to be trained, instructed and moulded by Higgins to give the outward impression of a duchess: now she must find her true identity for herself.

Her rebellion in Act Four is the beginning of that process and it is completed during the confrontation with Higgins at the end of Act Five. When the conversation begins, she does not know how it will end, but she has to battle with Higgins for her independence. With his verbal skill, his self-confidence and his refusal to make any concessions, Eliza's task of breaking free from his domination is formidable. For much of the conversation, Eliza demands that Higgins acknowledge her as a person by some show of personal feelings. Several remarks illustrate this: 'I dont care how you treat me . . . But I wont be passed over' (p. 126); 'I wont care for anybody that doesnt care for me' (p. 127); 'What did you do it for, if you didnt care for me?' and 'I notice that you dont notice me' (p. 128). Only when she realizes that she can get all the personal, human response she longs for from Freddy and that by becoming a teacher she can support them both, is her dependence on Higgins broken. Now, truly herself, she is on equal terms with Higgins – and can leave him.

## ALFRED DOOLITTLE

Alfred Doolittle appears only twice in the play – at the very beginning of Eliza's attempt to change her whole life and at the end, just before her final success. Like his daughter's, Doolittle's life undergoes a remarkable change after meeting Professor Higgins, but the outcome is very different. Eliza finds independence and the door to a new and fuller life: Doolittle finds himself miserable and bound hand and foot by middle-class morality.

The stage direction on page 53 introduces us to this 'elderly but vigorous dustman'. Shaw tells us he 'seems equally free from fear and conscience'. He is certainly not troubled by conscience when he comes to sell his daughter for five pounds. He is an engaging rogue, rejoicing in what he regards as his freedom and surviving on his skill at 'talking money out of other people's pockets into his own'. Eliza is ashamed that he works as a dustman when he can earn good money as a navvy, which is his proper job (p. 62). But Doolittle has chosen to be one of the undeserving poor. This means that he flouts the rules of middle-class morality, going his own way and living regardless of others. The penalty for this is that he can never receive the charity given to the deserving poor, who, outwardly at least, conform to middle-class standards of right and wrong. Doolittle resents this but still feels that his way of life is 'the only one that has any ginger in it'.

He has a natural gift for words: 'I'm willing to tell you. I'm wanting to tell you. I'm waiting to tell you' (p. 55). His long speech on middle-class morality (p. 58) so impresses Higgins that he says with three months' training Doolittle could choose between a seat in the cabinet and a 'popular pulpit' in Wales. But Doolittle has considered all this (for he claims to be a 'thinking man') and has rejected politics, religion and social reform, along with 'all the other amusements' in favour of undeserving poverty.

His attitude to women is a mixture of scorn and fascination. He tells Higgins to marry Eliza because, 'If you dont youll be sorry for it after. If you do, s h e 'll be sorry for it after; but better her than you, because youre a man, and she's only a woman and dont know how to be happy anyhow' (p. 60). Yet women get their own back on him because he is so susceptible to their charms. According to Eliza (p.43), she has had six 'stepmothers'. No wonder Doolittle laments, 'I have been the victim of one woman after another all my life . . .' (p. 125). Such a woman is too wise to marry him and give him a hold over her. Instead, as he admits, 'I got to be agreeable to her. I got to give her presents. I got to buy her clothes something sinful. I'm a slave to that woman, Governor, just because I'm not her lawful husband' (pp. 59, 60). He is a natural courtier where women are concerned. Notice how he stands aside and apologizes when he meets Eliza (whom he does not recognize) in the doorway (p. 60) and how courteously and deferentially he talks to Mrs Higgins (p. 114). In a letter sent to the actor who was rehearsing the part of Doolittle for the first London production in 1914, Shaw wrote, 'Adapt yourself to Mrs Higgins's presence and throw yourself with instinctive good manners and the gallantry that has made you a slave to women all your life, on her sympathy . . . the dustman has much more social talent than anyone present . . . Doolittle is a born genius at the game . . .'

This talent will no doubt stand Doolittle in good stead when he has to move in high society, thanks to his inheritance of the Wannafeller fortune. As Higgins says to Eliza, '. . . your father is not a snob . . . and . . . will be quite at home in any station of life to which his eccentric destiny may call him'. But Doolittle is miserable at the prospect. Fear of the workhouse in his old age denies him the liberty to give up the fortune that he does not want. As a result, his freedom is lost. He must conform to middle-class ways of behaviour, must marry his 'missus' (though neither desires it) and he must support the many professional men, servants and relatives who will crowd around him because of his wealth. In contrast to Eliza, whose vitality is liberated when she leaves Higgins, Doolittle's vitality is sapped now that this essentially irresponsible man is forced to 'live for others' (p. 116). He goes off to his wedding, a ridiculous figure in his middle-class finery, thoroughly unhappy that the middle-class morality he had always hated has now claimed him as its victim.

## THE EYNSFORD HILLS

In a play in which many social grades are represented, from ambassador to dustman, the Eynsford Hills illustrate the most depressing situation of all: those with social position but no money to support it. They are the most useless members of the middle class, despised even by their own class, as we see from the few invitations to parties that Clara receives (p. 80). Their lives are spent in a vapid round of social calls; neither son nor daughter has a job, nor the ability to find one.

Mrs Eynsford Hill is a sad and gentle creature, dominated and bullied by Clara, but quietly fond of her son: 'But the boy is nice. Dont you think so?' (p. 80). She admits to her old friend Mrs Higgins that they are poor and her eyes are moist as she thinks of the lack of opportunity this means for her children. Of course she is startled by Eliza's conversation and shocked by her 'Not bloody likely'. She accepts the explanation about the new small talk but does not really approve. She finds the fashionable expressions of young people 'horrible and unladylike' and is horrified when Clara adopts Eliza's language.

Clara is an unpleasant girl but perhaps she elicits a little sympathy because her social background and lack of money have placed her in an impossible situation. She accompanies her mother on the pointless round of at-homes – and to the rare party – determined to be fashionable in talk and behaviour but with very little idea of what these really are. She is completely taken in by Higgins telling her to use the new small talk at the three at-homes she is to attend. 'Pitch it in strong', he tells her (p. 79). One dreads to think of the reception she will get.

We first meet Clara at the very beginning of the play (p. 13), complaining about Freddy's inability to find a taxi. When he arrives without one a little later she roundly calls him 'a selfish pig'. She tries to tell her mother not to buy a flower from Eliza and criticizes her conversation with the girl. She reacts violently when Higgins dares to identify her as coming from 'Earlscourt'. In this first scene she is consistently ill-tempered.

When she visits Mrs Higgins's at-home her manner is bright and social. She flirtatiously tries to get on good terms with Professor Higgins, sympathizing with him for his lack of small talk, but she only succeeds in provoking from him a crushing denunciation of the ignorance of this so-called civilized and cultured class of society. She is very impressed with Eliza, moving to sit beside her on the ottoman and 'devouring her with her eyes' (p. 75). Her brisk rebuttal of her mother's doubts about the new ways of speaking leads Mrs Eynsford Hill to bring their visit to an end. But, encouraged by Higgins in a wicked mood, Clara departs 'radiant, conscious of being thoroughly up to date'.

Freddy is simply a very likeable young man, with little to recommend him except pleasant manners and (we presume) good looks. He is infatuated with Eliza from the first moment of their meeting and offers her complete devotion ever after. In the film extract (p. 106), he tells Eliza that he spends most of his nights outside her house as it is the only place where he is happy! Higgins regards him with the utmost contempt: 'that young fool! That poor devil who couldnt get a job as an errand boy even if he had the guts to try for it! (p. 131). It is no compliment to him when Eliza says, 'I'll marry Freddy, I will, as soon as I'm able to support him'. But Freddy's importance to Eliza lies in one simple fact: 'Freddy loves me: that makes him king enough for me'. She goes on to say that she does not want him to work, for he was not brought up to it as she was. Freddy can supply the simple warm human feeling that Higgins will not offer her and this is sufficient for Eliza. In the play, Eliza's development into a fully liberated woman is made absolutely clear by her marrying this weak young man who will be utterly dependent on her.

## MRS PEARCE

Mrs Pearce is Professor Higgins's housekeeper and she steers a difficult course between being a respectful servant and a mother-substitute. She has been with Higgins long enough to be quite firm with him when necessary. When she is told to bath Eliza and burn her clothes (p. 41), she begins to protest and is soon insisting, 'You must be reasonable, Mr Higgins . . . You cant walk over everybody like this'. She dismisses Higgins's extravagant forecast that the streets will be strewn with the bodies of men shooting themselves for Eliza's sake with a brisk, 'Nonsense, sir. You mustnt talk to her like that'. When Higgins calls Eliza 'an ungrateful wicked girl', Mrs Pearce throws it back at him: 'Stop, Mr Higgins. I wont allow it. It's you that are wicked' (p. 43). She is clearly a force to be reckoned with in the household. She is also the first person in the play to put the question concerning Eliza: 'And what is to become of her when youve finished your teaching?' (p. 44). Needless to say, Mrs Pearce does not get a satisfactory answer, but she has been the first to articulate the central question of the play.

Her role as a mother-substitute comes out most clearly in the amusing scene on pages 50–52. Dramatically, its function is to allow time for Eliza to bath and dress, but Shaw creates an amusing comedy out of the implacable Mrs Pearce rebuking her master for his swearing, his carelessness over his dress and his indifferent table manners, thereby forcing him on to the defensive for once. But Mrs Pearce is also aware of Higgins's skill in getting his own way through charm and cajolery. Eliza refers to this in Act Five (p. 127) where she says, 'Mrs Pearce warned me. Time and again she has wanted to leave you; and you always got round her at the last minute. And you dont care a bit for her . . .' Being housekeeper to Professor Higgins cannot be easy, but Mrs Pearce strikes us as a very sensible, capable woman quite equal to her task.

## NEPOMMUCK

Nepommuck is the only character introduced into the film sequences who is of any interest. His is an amusing cameo role, the hairy-faced young man so full of his own importance and confident that he is Higgins's most famous pupil. He is quite unabashed at Higgins's failure to recognize him. He takes Higgins's rude remark, 'Why dont you shave?', as a question to be taken quite seriously and replies that his whiskers are a substitute for Higgins's imposing appearance. He is thoroughly at home in the exalted circles in which he moves, the eternal courtier toadying to the nobility and searching out secrets on their behalf.

At the ambassador's reception he is employed as an interpreter, for he speaks thirty-two languages. He says of the Greek diplomatist (who pretends he cannot speak English, despite being the son of a Clerkenwell watchmaker), 'I help him pretend; but I make him pay through the nose. I make them all pay. Ha Ha!' (pp. 90–91). His profession is similar to Higgins's in that he too helps social upstarts to disguise their origins, and he is skilled at placing people by their accents. We may assume he also teaches English pronunciation, for Eliza declares she will work as his assistant when she becomes a teacher.

Although Higgins is contemptuous of Nepommuck, he has to take him seriously: 'If he finds her out I lose my bet'. In the event, Nepommuck fails to identify Eliza correctly and his false judgement wins the bet for Higgins. His presence in the scene brings drama and uncertainty to Eliza's appearance at the ambassador's reception and eventually clinches her triumph. His boastful confidence in his own opinion serves to intensify the hollowness of the social pretensions and the ways of this world of high society. It is significant that Nepommuck calls himself 'the marvellous boy' (p. 89). This was the phrase applied by Wordsworth to Thomas Chatterton (1752–70), the young poet famous for his poetic forgeries!

# Commentary

## THE LEGEND OF PYGMALION

Shaw takes the title of his play from a legendary king of Cyprus named Pygmalion, a man widely famed as a sculptor. His masterpiece was the statue of a woman, whom he named Galatea. She was so beautiful that Pygmalion fell in love with her. He begged Aphrodite, the goddess of love, to bring the statue to life and give her to him as his bride. The goddess granted his request; the statue came to life and Pygmalion married his Galatea.

*Pygmalion* is therefore an apposite title for the play, but only up to a point. Professor Higgins is the Pygmalion figure and his achievement parallels that of the sculptor in that he creates a real woman from unpromising material. (To what extent the change was entirely due to him is discussed in the character study of Higgins, pp. 50–55). Yet the classical legend is a love story. Pygmalion falls in love with his creation and marries her, whereas Higgins resolutely refuses any romantic connection with Eliza – and she with him. The profound difference between Pygmalion and Higgins is that the former created a woman who was to be bound to him for life, whereas Higgins's creation became entirely independent of him.

## TO SPEAK LIKE A LADY...

Higgins explains his attitude about training Eliza to speak like a lady to his mother at the end of Act Three (pp. 81–2): 'But you have no idea how frightfully interesting it is to take a human being and change her into a quite different human being by creating a new speech for her. It's filling up the deepest gulf that separates class from class and soul from soul.'

This ambitious programme is hardly borne out in the play. By the time Eliza has won the bet for him she has become a well-trained 'doll'. Her rebellion and her search for her own independence create the real woman. Higgins, too, learns a great deal from the experience, realizing very early on that there is more to it than simply teaching pronunciation: 'You see the difficulty? . . . To get her to talk grammar. The mere pronunciation is easy enough' (p. 44). A little later, in Act Three, he tells his mother, '. . . you have to consider not only how a girl pronounces but what she pronounces . . .' (p. 70). At the end of this act he acknowledges that Eliza's soul has caught his interest too: 'I'm worn out thinking about her, and watching her lips and her teeth and her tongue, not to mention her soul, which is the quaintest of the lot' (p. 81).

In Act Five Higgins admits to Eliza that he has learnt something from her 'idiotic notions' (p. 127) and a few lines later, in reply to Eliza's suggestion that when he feels lonely without her, he can turn on a recording of her voice, he remarks, 'I can't turn your soul on'. So Higgins is forced to admit that there is much more to changing a human being than simply 'creating a new speech for her'.

The upstarts whom Higgins (and Nepommuck) train have already risen in society because of their ability to make money. Training them to speak middle-class English merely disguises their origins for social and business purposes. Eliza's approach was different from theirs. She hoped that refined speech would gain her a job in a flower shop. In the event, she did turn into 'a quite different human being' by first being a dutiful pupil and then by rebelling against her teacher.

## MONEY AND SOCIETY

Money plays an important part in *Pygmalion*. On it depends Higgins's freedom to live and behave as he pleases. Doolittle, with a little money occasionally, can enjoy life as one of the undeserving poor; given a larger sum his happiness is destroyed. Eliza comes from abject poverty to find her soul, but cannot become free to live her own life until she sees a way of earning money as a teacher. The Eynsford Hills drag out a grey existence in a class where money is taken for granted, yet they are too poor to do any more than keep up appearances. But for Mrs Higgins money is no problem and she enjoys a secure life in middle-class comfort.

In each case, money is linked to social position. As a flower girl, Eliza, who has to survive on a few shillings a day, is a figure of abject poverty, a 'draggletailed guttersnipe' with no prospects whatsoever. On the social scale she is among the lowest of the low. Her father is also a slum dweller; he finds his answer to life in the limited happiness to be attained by scrounging money for drink and in abandoning all sense of responsibility. There is thus a great social gulf in the play between Eliza and her father and the other characters.

Status in society is decided by money. Once Doolittle is given a fortune, he automatically becomes a member of the middle classes – and very unhappy about it, too. Eliza herself is placed in a most curious and unusual situation: for six months she has lived as a member of the middle class and has been trained to speak and behave like one. As a result she feels it would be impossible for her to return to her life in the slums: 'You know I cant go back to the gutter . . . You know well I couldnt bear to live with a low common man after you two . . .' (p. 131). But she has no means of surviving independently in this class, since she has no money of her own. As soon as she realizes how she can earn money her problem is solved.

Social position based on wealth is shown to be a sham. The clearest denunciation of it comes with Higgins's scathing attack on the ignorance of the middle classes (p. 73): 'You see, we're all savages, more or less . . .' But the sham is also shown in the ludicrous figure of Doolittle dressed for his wedding in the morning suit of the middle-class gentleman; this dress very obviously does not reflect the inner man. The Eynsford Hills also reveal the hollowness of social class. Freddy, as Eliza says, has not been brought up to earn his living and is weak and useless. His mother and sister pass their time in idle visits and pointless conversation. Even in the highest ranks of society there is hollowness. The ambassador's party shows how a slum girl, properly trained, can convince anyone she is a duchess and this raises the question of what true merit there can be in being one of the upper classes. Higgins has no doubt when he speaks of his dinner companion: 'The dinner was worse: sitting gorging there for over an hour, with nobody but a damned fool of a fashionable woman to talk to!' (pp. 98–9). Yet he makes his living in this 'age of upstarts' by training people who rise in the world to disguise their origins (p. 27).

The possession of money often brings quite unmerited power and position. It enables the middle class to impose its standards of morality on others (unless, like Doolittle, they choose to be 'undeserving') and it gives them freedom of action denied to the poor, as Eliza knows too well.

For Professor Higgins, money enables him to live his own life in his own way; it permits him to be bad-mannered and overbearing. Its beneficial effects are shown in Mrs Higgins, who lives what appears to be a calm and satisfying life, gracious to her friends, wise and supportive to her son.

It is significant that *Pygmalion* begins with a group of people from all classes of society sheltering from the rain in the portico of St Paul's church; it is as if to show that all men are equal in the eyes of God and that nature has no respect for class. But class distinctions are revealed as soon as conversation begins, for each class has its distinctive accent. Eliza's anxiety to earn a few pence for her flowers is contrasted with the way Higgins recklessly throws a handful of coins into her basket.

At the end of *Pygmalion* we emerge with no respect for a class system based on the possession (or lack) of money. Yet we see that money does enable a person of ability and independence of mind to be truly classless, as Higgins is when he speaks of 'having the same manner for all human souls . . . behaving as if you were in Heaven, where there are no third-class carriages, and one soul is as good as another' (p. 126). Eliza leaves the stage with this strength and ability to be free and classless, living her own life confidently, whatever course it might take in the years ahead.

## STRUCTURE

Act One serves as a prologue to the play; we are introduced to five of the principal characters and hear Professor Higgins's proud boast, upon which the rest of the play is based.

Act Two motivates the play, with Eliza taking the first steps towards self-improvement by coming to the Professor's house to ask for lessons, and Pickering making the bet with Higgins about passing her off as a duchess. We also have the first of Doolittle's two appearances. The question of Eliza's future is raised by Mrs Pearce but Higgins is not interested.

Act Three shows the progress that has been made in Eliza's training. While it is obvious that she is not yet ready to pass as a lady, she has certainly made enough progress in a short time to indicate that she will eventually win Higgins's bet for him. The scene shows the somewhat unreal character of Eliza being produced by Higgins's training, though her racy conversation reminds us of the true Eliza beneath the veneer of good elocution and proper deportment. The question of Eliza's future is raised again and more urgently by Mrs Higgins, but still without result.

Act Four is quite a short one and it concentrates on Eliza's rebellion. The experiment is over, her future very uncertain and her feelings deeply hurt. Eliza can stand it no longer. She signals her revolt by throwing Higgins's slippers at him and later by leaving his house; but at this point she does not know how she can survive for any length of time without him. Although she knows she must become independent, she does not yet know how to achieve this.

Early in Act Five, Doolittle makes his second appearance, ironically paralleling his daughter's own rise in the world. The climax of the whole play is the confrontation between Eliza and Higgins, in the course of which she finally discovers how to break free from him.

## PARALLELS AND CONTRASTS

A fascinating aspect of *Pygmalion* is the number of parallels and contrasts to be seen among the characters. The most noticeable is the similarity of situation between Eliza and Doolittle. Both come out of the slums to visit Higgins, Eliza to seek a new and fuller life, her father (quite happy where he is) to 'touch' Higgins for a fiver. Yet the result of the meeting is as dramatic for him as for Eliza. In the time that it takes for Eliza to become an independent woman, Doolittle inherits a fortune and enters the middle class. But the contrast is illuminating. Doolittle has gained wealth he does not really want and his happiness is destroyed; Eliza has gained freedom of action and the possibility of supporting herself in her new life. Her freedom and independent spirit bring her new opportunities but her father, who never wanted to rise above his poverty, is handed over to the middle-class morality he hates.

There are also valid comparisons to be made between Doolittle and Higgins. Eliza notes the parallel both when she responds to Higgins's bullying in Act Two, 'One would think you was my father' (p. 40), and in Act Five, 'The same to every body . . . like father' (p. 126). Higgins grinningly accepts that there may be something in the comparison, and remarks that Doolittle is not a snob and will be at home in any station in life. Both men flout convention, shock those who are hidebound by rules of behaviour and insist on the freedom to lead their lives in their own way. Both men are gifted speakers and possessèd of a disarming charm. Doolittle's freedom depends on complete – and undeserving – poverty, while Higgins's freedom is based on financial security. In their different situations each man can do as he likes. It is ironic that when Doolittle becomes a rich man, he loses his freedom and his happiness completely. Money forces him to become 'responsible', something totally against his nature. Higgins, however, with enough money to live very comfortably, can devote himself to his own scientific pursuits, sustained by an abstract belief in the value of life and humanity in general, and cushioned from the world by Mrs Higgins and Mrs Pearce.

These two women have parallel roles in the play, sharing between them the duties of being a mother to Higgins. His natural mother lives in her own house but is frequently visited by her son, who regards her as his ideal woman. She can advise, counsel and admonish him as necessary, but is removed from the hurly-burly of life in the same house as he. This is the fate of Mrs Pearce, who has to put up with his swearing, his temper and his table manners. She has to clean the lapels of his dressing-gown when he has wiped his fingers on them and put away the clothes he tosses over the banisters. Like a mother with a badly behaved child, she feels she has the right to speak sharply to him and sometimes – as in Act Two (pp. 50–52) – to rebuke him roundly. The poor woman has a great deal to put up with and it is no wonder that she has tried to leave his service a number of times, but with the charm that a spoilt child can often display he has always persuaded her to stay.

A woman of similar social position to Mrs Higgins is her old friend, Mrs Eynsford Hill. Yet the contrast between the two women is striking. Mrs Eynsford Hill is a poor creature, dragged down by the misery of genteel poverty. In this play where money and social position are central themes, she represents the unhappiest situation of all – social position without the money to support it. Mrs Higgins lives comfortably and at ease with the world, able to deal with the bad manners of her son and in control of the unusual situations that develop in her drawing room in Acts Three and Five. Mrs Eynsford Hill, however, is a victim of her lack of money and is burdened with an unpleasant daughter and a charming but useless son, himself a total contrast in intellect and ability to Professor Higgins.

Apart from Eliza, the only other girl in the play is Clara Eynsford Hill. Although her role is a small one, she too provides interesting contrasts. Whereas Eliza, rising from the slums, seeks and eventually finds a full and satisfying independent life, Clara starts with the advantage of social position but seems doomed to a life of frustration and disappointment. She tries to compensate for her insecurity by excessive brightness and a desperation to be fashionable, as with her response to Higgins's mock-serious suggestion that she take up the new small talk. Unlike Eliza, Clara is prepared to flirt with Higgins. The stage direction on page 73 tells us she 'considers Higgins quite eligible matrimonially' and she tries to chat with him on equal terms. But Higgins simply denounces her class. Unlike Eliza she seems condemned to continue her life of empty social rounds.

Shaw has given Professor Higgins a companion whose interests and social class parallel his own, but whose attitude and manners afford a distinct contrast. Pickering is drawn to Higgins as a fellow expert in the field of spoken language; each admires the other's work. The ease with which they strike up a friendship in Act One and go off to sup together shows their very similar backgrounds. But Colonel Pickering is a traditional English gentleman who will straighten himself in the presence of a woman – even the housekeeper (p. 36) – and will offer the flower girl a chair and address her as Miss Doolittle. Eliza believes she learnt to be a lady more from Pickering's good manners than from Higgins's lessons, during which she was alternately bullied and cajoled.

A final parallel may be drawn between the character of Nepommuck from the film sequences and that of Higgins. Nepommuck is also a speech expert and capable of placing people by their accents. He too earns his living by helping people to disguise their humble origins. Higgins tells Pickering (p. 27) that he himself earns a living ('Quite a fat one') in 'this age of upstarts' by teaching men who are rising in the world. Nepommuck boasts of his success as an interpreter and of the way he is helping a Greek diplomat (really the son of a Clerkenwell watchmaker) to disguise the speech of his humble origins by a pretence of neither speaking nor understanding English. Both men make us feel that social position is a sham.

## PREFACE (*pp. 5–9*)

Shaw was famous for the long prefaces he wrote for his plays. These are usually extended essays discussing the general issues raised in the plays and can be considered quite separately from the plays themselves. The preface to *Pygmalion* is very short by Shaw's standards and adds little or nothing to our understanding of the play. It is mostly devoted to Shaw's views on the phonetics expert, Henry Sweet. He denies that Higgins is a portrait of Sweet, though he admits that there are touches of Sweet in the play. In his final paragraph (p. 9), Shaw suggests that Eliza's change of speech is not at all unusual and that thousands of people have acquired a new accent.

## EPILOGUE (*pp. 134–48*)

The sequel to the play is far more extensive than the Preface and much more interesting. The play is of course complete without it and needs no epilogue for a full understanding of the story and its implications. However, we all like to wonder what happens to characters when a play ends and Shaw decided to satisfy the curiosity of those who read the play. It also enabled Shaw to show how Eliza survived independently of Higgins and as the wife of Freddy.

On pages 134–7 Shaw is at pains to show just why Eliza saw that Higgins would not be a suitable husband for her. He says 'she was instinctively aware that she could never obtain a complete grip of him or come between him and his mother' and she knew that interest in herself would come second to his philosophic interests. Moreover, her resentment of his 'domineering superiority' and his way of getting round her when he had gone too far in his bullying re-inforced her instinct against marrying him.

The possibilities for a successful marriage between a weak young man and a strong-willed girl are discussed on pages 137 and 138. The complications in Eliza's marriage to Freddy are financial ones and from page 138 onwards Shaw sketches out what happened to Eliza and Freddy, as well as to Doolittle and to Clara Eynsford Hill. His account is interesting and entertaining and is well worth reading, providing you treat it as something separate from the play itself. *Pygmalion* was written for the theatre and neither Preface nor Epilogue has anything to do with the theatrical experience.

# Glossary

| | |
|---|---|
| *Alliteration:* | words in a sequence beginning with the same letter |
| *Arbitrary:* | domineering |
| *At-home:* | period set aside by a hostess for social calls to her house |
| *Barmy:* | mad |
| *Bee in her bonnet:* | to have an obsessive, fixed idea |
| *Benzine:* | petroleum derivative used to remove grease |
| *Billet-doux:* | a brief love letter |
| *Blackguard:* | rogue |
| *Brougham:* | coach or car for two to four persons |
| *Brusquely:* | abruptly |
| *Chaperoned:* | escorted and protected (usually applied to a young girl) |
| *Charybdis:* | in Greek legend, a whirlpool on one side of the narrow Straits of Messina between Sicily and Italy. Opposite was the monster Scylla. Together they form a proverb suggesting the difficulty of choosing between two unpleasant alternatives. See *Skilly* |
| *Condescension:* | courtesy to one's inferiors |
| *Consort battleship:* | battleship which accompanies another vessel |
| *Copper:* | (1) policeman, (2) water boiler |
| *Decorum:* | politeness |
| *Drudge:* | over-worked servant |
| *Eccentric:* | odd, peculiar |
| *Estheticism:* | pretence to a love of the Arts |
| *Half a crown:* | two shillings and sixpence (12½p) |
| *Hanwell:* | district in London with a lunatic asylum |
| *Imprecations:* | curses |
| *Incorrigible:* | beyond reform |
| *Intimidated:* | frightened |
| *Kimono:* | loose Japanese robe |
| La Fanciulla del Golden West: | *The Girl of the Golden West*, an opera by Puccini (1858–1924) |

| | |
|---|---|
| *Maestro:* | master |
| *Magnanimous:* | generous, unselfish |
| *Mendacity:* | lying |
| *Molestation:* | annoyance, interference with |
| *Monkey Brand:* | a strong kitchen soap |
| *Moralist:* | teacher of what is right and wrong |
| *Morganatic:* | refers to a marriage between a royal person and a woman of inferior rank, who does not share her husband's titles |
| *Morris:* | William Morris (1834–96), an influential designer, craftsman and poet. Friend of the artist Burne-Jones |
| *Mrs Langtry:* | famed Edwardian actress and beauty |
| *Nark:* | informer |
| *Navvy:* | labourer on road construction, etc |
| *Nectar:* | wine of the gods |
| *Ottoman:* | sofa |
| *Pandour:* | fierce Hungarian foot-soldier |
| *Pauperize:* | to make dependent on charity |
| *Pedantic:* | insisting on the importance of trivial details |
| *Perfunctorily:* | done mechanically and neglectfully |
| *Presumptuous:* | behaving impertinently |
| *Prudery:* | exaggerated modesty |
| *Rhetoric:* | art of speech-making |
| *Rossettian:* | in the style of a painting by Dante Gabriel Rossetti (1828–82) |
| *Sanguinary:* | bloody |
| *Skilly:* | see *Charybdis*; also thin soup served in a workhouse |
| *Small talk:* | social conversation on trivial topics |
| *Soirée:* | social meeting held in the evening |
| *Somnambulist:* | sleep-walker |
| *Subjective:* | influenced by one's own thoughts |
| *Sumptuous:* | very luxurious |
| *Togs:* | clothes |
| *'Turned off':* | slang expression for 'hanged' |
| *voluble:* | very talkative |
| *Whitely:* | a well-known shop |

# Examination Questions

1.  Read the following passage, and answer all the questions printed beneath it:

MRS EYNSFORD HILL [*suffering from shock*] Well, I really cant get used to the new ways.

CLARA [*throwing herself discontentedly into the Elizabethan chair*] Oh, it's all right, mamma, quite right. People will think we never go anywhere or see anybody if you are so old-fashioned.  5

MRS EYNSFORD HILL. I daresay I am very old-fashioned; but I do hope you wont begin using that expression, Clara. I have got accustomed to hear you talking about men as rotters, and calling everything filthy and beastly; though I do think it horrible and unladylike. But this last is really too much. Dont you think so, Colonel  10
Pickering?

PICKERING. Dont ask me. Ive been away in India for several years; and manners have changed so much that I sometimes dont know whether I'm at a respectable dinner-table or in a ship's forecastle.  15

CLARA. It's all a matter of habit. Theres no right or wrong in it. Nobody means anything by it. And it's so quaint, and gives such a smart emphasis to things that are not in themselves very witty. I find the new small talk delightful and quite innocent.

MRS EYNSFORD HILL [*rising*] Well, after that, I think it's time  20
for us to go.

*Pickering and Higgins rise.*

CLARA [*rising*] Oh yes: we have three at-homes to go to still. Goodbye, Mrs Higgins. Goodbye, Colonel Pickering. Goodbye, Professor Higgins.  25

HIGGINS [*coming grimly at her from the divan, and accompanying her to the door*] Goodbye. Be sure you try on that small talk at the three at-homes. Dont be nervous about it. Pitch it in strong.

CLARA [*all smiles*] I will. Goodbye. Such nonsense, all this early
Victorian prudery!                                                     30

(i) Describe briefly what takes place immediately before this
extract.

(ii) Explain *I sometimes dont . . . forecastle* (lines 13–15) and *gives
such . . . very witty* (lines 17 and 18).

(iii) Why is the episode of which the extract is a part so important
to Higgins and Eliza?

(iv) Give a brief account of the conversation between Higgins,
Pickering and Mrs Higgins after her callers have gone.


2. Read the following passage, and answer all the questions printed
beneath it:

MRS HIGGINS. But, my dear Mr Doolittle, you need not suffer
all this if you are really in earnest. Nobody can force you to
accept this bequest. You can repudiate it. Isnt that so, Colonel
Pickering?

PICKERING. I do believe so.                                            5

DOOLITTLE [*softening his manner in deference to her sex*] Thats the
tragedy of it, maam. It's easy to say chuck it; but I havnt the nerve.
Which of us has? We're all intimidated. Intimidated, maam: thats
what we are. What is there for me if I chuck it but the workhouse in
my old age? I have to dye my hair already to keep my job as a          10
dustman. If I was one of the deserving poor, and had put by a bit, I
could chuck it; but then why should I, acause the deserving poor
might as well be millionaires for all the happiness they ever has. They
dont know what happiness is. But I, as one of the undeserving poor,
have nothing between me and the pauper's uniform but this here        15
blasted three thousand a year that shoves me into the middle class.
(Excuse the expression, maam; youd use it yourself if you had my
provocation.) Theyve got you every way you turn: it's a choice between
the Skilly of the workhouse and the Char Bydis of the middle class;
and I havnt the nerve for the workhouse. Intimidated: thats what I     20
am. Broke. Bought up. Happier men than me will call for my dust,
and touch me for their tip; and I'll look on helpless, and envy them.
And thats what your son has brought me to. [*He is overcome by
emotion.*]

MRS HIGGINS. Well, I'm very glad youre not going to do anything   25
foolish, Mr Doolittle. For this solves the problem of Eliza's future.
You can provide for her now.

(i) State briefly where in the play this extract occurs.
(ii) Give the meaning of: *Intimidated* (line 8); *provocation* (line 18);
*Skilly of the workhouse* and the *Char Bydis of the middle class*
(line 19).
(iii) Explain *And thats what your son has brought me to* (line 23).
(iv) Bring out the humour of this extract.
                    (*University of Oxford Local Examination Board, 1972*)


3. 'His manner varies from genial bullying when he is in a good
humour to stormy petulance when anything goes wrong; but he is so
entirely frank and void of malice that he remains likeable even in
his least reasonable moments.' Show whether you agree with this
description of Professor Higgins.
                    (*University of Oxford Local Examination Board, 1972*)


4. Describe the changes Higgins brings about in Eliza during the
time she is his pupil, showing, by close reference to the play, whether
you think Eliza's basic character is changed.
                    (*Welsh Joint Education Committee, 1981*)


5. Identify yourself with Eliza Doolittle. What would your feelings
be if you had experienced what occurred to her from the time of
being met in Covent Garden to the time she returned from the ball?
Refer closely to incidents and characters in the play.
                    (*Welsh Joint Education Committee, 1981*)


6. Why did Shaw include Doolittle, Eliza's father, in *Pygmalion*?
How much did you enjoy his appearances?
(*Northern Ireland General Certificate of Education Examinations, 1983*)


7. Discuss Colonel Pickering's importance in the play. How interesting do you find him?
(*Northern Ireland General Certificate of Education Examinations, 1984*)